"The ability to deliver training online is essential for companies large and small. *The Learning Explosion* is an insightful and practical guide for making the virtual training move—a must-have for your training toolkit."

—**Kathy Chill**
VP, Business Development
Citrix Online

"*The Learning Explosion* is a great resource for training professionals charged with the task of introducing virtual learning to a corporate environment. Whether you're incorporating a blended-learning approach or straight virtual-classroom training, the new mind-set and the new rule-set outlined in this book will serve as your go-to guide."

—**Paul Krause**
President and CEO
Element K

"The training world is changing. Don't go virtual on your own... let *The Learning Explosion* guide the way."

—**Andrew Scivally**
President
eLearning Brothers

# The
# Learning
# eXPLOSION

## Matthew Murdoch
## Treion Muller

ISBN 978-1-936111-21-3

Printed in the United States of America.

# Table of Contents

## Foreword

First and foremost, I am a teacher. Teaching is where I found my voice. I have dedicated myself to traveling around the world to teach timeless, universal principles and inspire people to fulfill their potential and their unique purpose and mission in life. From boardrooms and government chambers to classrooms, family rooms, and community halls, I have met people from all walks of life, from all four corners of the world. In each of these special engagements, I have been humbled by the transformational power of principle-based learning.

The pursuit of knowledge is an exciting process, and the speed and demand for learning is ever increasing, especially in our fast-changing world. Daily, we all search for answers to questions and problems as we face new challenges. With technological advances, a wealth of information is now available that can quench this thirst for knowledge and connect people for information sharing. Because of this technological network, there is vast and growing potential for learning to flow to all humankind. It is our opportunity and responsibility to help this knowledge flow reach learners so they can achieve their potential.

I am amazed at the different types of technology I am able to use to teach and instruct people around the world. Online delivery of lessons and content is allowing me to teach people I would never reach otherwise. This is very exciting. As a result of this real-time, on-demand learning, people have the ability to acquire insights quicker and immediately apply their learnings to their specific problems or opportunities.

There will always be a need for in-person interaction. Yet, for learning to occur, it does not need to happen solely in a classroom made of bricks and mortar. Learning is happening in your organization right now. People are finding sources of knowledge all around them on the Internet, in books, on a conference call, and in virtual classrooms. Although I will always enjoy physically shaking the hands of people and seeing the excitement in their eyes after they have obtained new knowledge, I believe we have reached a point in our lives where the act of learning has changed, and we need to accommodate people's needs.

This book will give you the principles and mind-set to understand how learning is changing and exploding. It will explain the way learners acquire information and how you can provide it to them through the use of a new virtual-classroom rule-set.

I encourage you to think through these concepts and use them to improve the reach and quality of your learning and teaching. I am thrilled to have this body of work and excited to be taking part in new learning technologies to make a greater contribution in the world.

*Stephen R. Covey*

Dr. Stephen R. Covey

## Introduction

When we started researching the feasibility of moving face-to-face training to virtual classrooms, we attended numerous online events and spoke to many experts. We then set out applying the best of what we heard and read and omitted the ineffective practices we experienced firsthand. Since then, we have actively been testing, modifying, retesting, and fine-tuning our virtual-classroom programs while training instructors and launching virtual-classroom initiatives worldwide.

The purpose of this book is to share the principles and practices we've discovered with everyone who has been tasked with moving traditional training to virtual classrooms.

**Virtual classroom** [vur-choo-uhl klas-room] -noun

A virtual classroom is a learning environment created in the virtual space. The objectives of virtual classrooms are to improve access to advanced educational experiences by allowing students and instructors to participate in remote learning communities using personal computers, and to improve the quality and effectiveness of education by using the computer to support a collaborative learning process. The explosion of the knowledge age has changed the context of what is learned and how it is learned--the concept of virtual classrooms is a manifestation of this knowledge revolution.[1]

Do we have all the answers, anecdotes, and instructions you will need? Probably not. But the rules, tools, and practical tips we share in this book will hopefully form a sound foundation from which to start or improve your own virtual-classroom initiative.

The first—and most important—learning principle we wish to share can be summarized in just three words: "Keep it short." Over the past decade, we have all been conditioned to learn in short, bite-size chunks, thanks to the billions of learning fragments available to us at the touch of a screen and with the click of a mouse. This is the new learning reality—the way most people want to learn, like to learn, and choose to learn.

You have probably noticed by now that we have followed our own advice. This book is fairly short. This was intentional. Think about how many times you have bought a business book, only to read the first couple of chapters and then put it away. We have been conditioned to read fast, to skim, and to find relevant nuggets.

Another valuable principle we have learned is to provide opportunities for learners to apply what they have just read. We have done this by providing a Learning Explosion Action Plan at the end of each chapter.

We recognize that all of us are at different stages of virtual-classroom development. And we all have varying needs and requirements. It is our hope and mission to provide you with new insight to help you succeed in this exciting and ever-changing modality of training.

From the blackboard to the Web;
from the desk to the virtual classroom;
from prescriptive instruction to self-directed;
from traditional to informal:
this is the new learning reality —
the way people want to learn, like to learn,
and choose to learn.


Understanding this ever-changing
learning dynamic will require a new mind-set
and a new rule-set.

# The
# New
# Mind-Set

# CHAPTER 1

# The Learning Explosion

**TWITTER SUMMARY ≤ 140 CHARACTERS**

A creative explosion is taking place. For the first time in history, pieces of knowledge and information are accessible to nearly everyone.

Right now, a teenager in Kobe, Japan, is learning a new skill on his mobile phone. A small-business owner in Sydney, Australia, is asking his professional network of online associates which Learning Management System (LMS) he should buy. A mother in Johannesberg, South Africa, is searching a medical website for how to treat her feverish child. A woman in Copenhagen, Denmark, is sharing information with others around the world through her blog, website, or wiki about a topic she is studying. Instantly, this piece of information—this learning fragment she has created—will generate interest in an online community. It will facilitate discussion. It will fuel new ideas, innovation, and learning. In this way, one learning fragment shared online will continue to explode.

We call this extraordinary event the Learning Explosion™.

## The Learning Explosion [the lur-ning ik-sploh-zhuhn] -noun

The perpetual explosion of knowledge into countless learning fragments. Fueled by ongoing technological advances, this explosion is resulting in the worldwide distribution of new ideas, innovation, and education.

## THE LEARNING EXPLOSION

Technological advances are taking the traditional learning model and breaking it into billions and billions of pieces of information that we now call learning fragments. In fact, all of us have probably discovered new learning fragments today. They are being created and discovered every minute of every hour. Learning is everywhere and accessible to nearly everyone. This is the new learning mind-set. This is how learning takes place today.

In your travels, you've probably witnessed the effects of the explosion firsthand. For instance, in 2009, while in the villages outside New Delhi, we saw some of the poorest people in the world accessing information on mobile phones. We've seen this same phenomenon in other parts of Asia, Central America, and Africa. The paradox is startling.

With tools like mobile phones and the Internet, information and knowledge is easily accessible to all classes of people worldwide. The Learning Explosion has no boundaries. This omnipresence of learning fragments allows for limitless opportunities to learn, grow, and increase your personal knowledge.

## The Catalysts That Sparked the Learning Explosion

But how did this Learning Explosion occur? It didn't happen overnight. In fact the catalysts have been evolving over half a millennium. A brief introduction to the catalysts and how they have changed the way we learn is beneficial as you begin to understand how to take your corporate learning online.

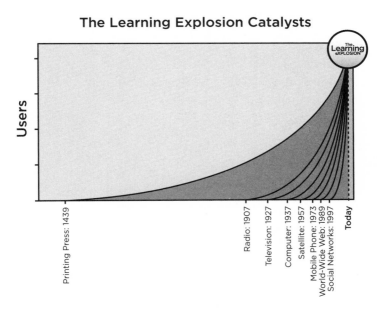

**The Learning Explosion Catalysts**

**Catalyst 1, Year: 1439.** While there may be some valid arguments for several earlier catalysts, we suggest the Learning Explosion can be traced back to a small German town when Johannes Gutenberg fired up the first printing press.

This first stage of learning evolution had the most profound impact of any of the stages, so much so that Gutenberg is considered the father of mass media. Mark Twain said this of Gutenberg: "What the world is to-day, good and bad, it owes to Gutenberg. Everything can be traced to this source, but we are bound to bring him homage...for the bad that his colossal invention has brought about is overshadowed a thousand times by the good with which mankind has been favored."

**Catalyst 2, Year: 1907.** Guglielmo Marconi successfully learned how to transmit and commercialize radio waves over extremely long distances.

**Catalyst 3, Year: 1927.** Philo T. Farnsworth developed the first working television system.

**Catalyst 4, Year: 1937.** The first computer was invented by George Stibitz at Bell Labs.

**Catalyst 5, Year: 1957.** The Soviet Union launched the first satellite, Sputnik, into orbit.

**Catalyst 6, Year: 1973.** The original cellular "brick phone" was invented by Martin Cooper at Motorola.

**Catalyst 7, Year: 1989.** Tim Berners-Lee established to-day's framework for the Internet—the World-Wide Web.

**Catalyst 8, Year: 1997.** The first social networking site, sixdegrees.com, is founded by Andrew Weinreich.

This list of catalysts will continue to grow over time. Although we don't know for sure what will occur next, we are assured that our quest for innovation will drive us further than we could every imagine.

**Learning Fragment**

**WIKIPEDIA.COM**

Search Wikipedia's open-source encyclopedia for a history of each of the eight catalysts, written collaboratively by volunteer contributors and online users. Most of the information shared also cites the source of that learning fragment, whether it be from a study, book, or other reference.

## The Explosion Is Growing

The abundance of research overwhelmingly supports the Learning Explosion's influence in the move to the virtual classroom and other online-learning platforms. Consider, for a moment, the number of people with access to the Internet. Based on ITU data, in 2010, the number of Internet users will surpass the 2 billion mark, of which 1.2 billion will be in developing countries. Usage has actually doubled between 2005 and 2010.[2] Plus, worldwide Wi-Fi coverage has grown over 155 percent since 2006.[3]

As younger generations enter the workforce, we will see a widespread shift in the way workers want to learn. In a 2010 report, the U.S. Department of Education estimated that more than one million students from kindergarten to Grade 12 were enrolled in online courses in 2007. The study also found that students in an online-learning format actually tended to outperform students learning in a classroom environment, earned higher grades, and displayed an overall greater understanding of the course materials.[4]

In just a few years, these students will be filling the offices of your organization. Are you ready for them? If not, be proactive and find out how you can be prepared.

Corporate America is also seeing a big jump in the use of virtual classrooms. For example, their usage increased from 45 percent in 2008 to 59 percent in 2009.[5]

The Learning Explosion is showing no signs of slowing down. In fact we see just the opposite—it will continue to speed up and grow exponentially. New statistics, research, and reports continue to support this. To get an idea of how the Learning Explosion has impacted you, take a moment to complete the technological self-assessment on pages 11 and 12.

## Learning Fragments

### LIST OF RESEARCH SOURCES

Here are just some of the many learning-fragment sources to which we have turned to learn about research and trends associated with the Learning Explosion and virtual classrooms, specifically.

- Pew Institute[6]—Publications on Internet and Technology
- ASTD[7]—Annual State of the Industry Report
- The eLearning Guild[8]—Annual Reports and White Papers
- Bersin & Associates—Annual Corporate Learning Factbook
- International Telecommunications Union (ITU)—White Paper, "The World in 2010: ICT Facts & Figures"
- Sloan Consortium[9]—Annual Online Learning Surveys
- Blackboard—Learning in the 21st Century Annual Report
- The National Broadband Plan[10]—Broadband Usage in the U.S. Report
- USDLA[11]—Education Research Reports
- The World Data Bank[12]—Data and Indicators on Almost Everything

## Learning Explosion Action Plan

### TECHNOLOGICAL SELF-ASSESSMENT

Place a check mark next to all the statements that apply to you. Then add up all the check marks and refer to the scoring key to find how you score on the Learning Explosion scale.

| | |
|---|---|
| ∅ | You have taken a picture of something interesting or funny just so that you can share it with your Facebook friends. |
| ∅ | You have used your mobile phone to find the answer to a tough question. |
| ○ | You have used Skype to talk to someone in another country. |
| ○ | You reach for your phone whenever you hear a chime. |
| ∅ | You have had a conversation with one person while texting another. |
| ○ | You claim Microsoft® Outlook® as your productivity tool. |
| ○ | You have not used a paper map in at least three years. |
| ○ | You have chosen a place to eat based on a stranger's recommendation found on an application on your mobile phone. |
| ∅ | You have felt the urge to criticize or praise a business through an application on your mobile phone. |
| ∅ | You pay your bills online. |
| ○ | You feel withdrawal symptoms if you leave your phone at home. |
| ○ | You own the domain for a personal URL. |
| ∅ | You "Google" to find the answer to everything. |
| ∅ | You have used YouTube to learn something new. |
| ○ | You have anxiously waited for a status update on a social network site from someone whom you have never met—like a celebrity on Twitter. |
| ∅ | You own an iPad, a Kindle, or other type of tablet. |

## Learning Explosion Action Plan

### TECHNOLOGICAL SELF-ASSESSMENT (CONT.)

○ You have started a group discussion on LinkedIn.

○ You frequently read someone else's blog.

○ You have stood in line for at least two hours to purchase a new "gadget."

○ You have contributed to a wiki of one kind or another.

| 8 | **Number of Check Marks** |

### SCORING KEY

How many statements did you check?

0–3   You must be living in a cave or studying tribes in the jungles of the Amazon.

4–9   Not bad, but you still have a long way to go.

10–15   You are starting to evolve quite nicely.

16–20   It looks like you have fully embraced the Learning Explosion. Kaboom!

# CHAPTER 2

# Learning Fragments

## TWITTER SUMMARY ≤ 140 CHARACTERS

Learning fragments are pieces of information accessible through Web-enabled devices or traditional offline media.

The Learning Explosion has forever altered how we learn. To help understand the impact of this event, ask yourself two simple questions:

1. "What problem did I have this week to which I didn't know the answer?"

2. Follow that with "Where did I find the answer?"

If you are like most people, you probably turned to one of your trusted learning-fragment sources like a favorite website or a mobile app. We doubt anyone drove to the nearest library, pulled down an *Encyclopedia Britannica*, and searched the pages to find the answer. If you did, we need to talk.

### Learning fragments [lur-ning frag-muhnt] -noun

Learning fragments are the result of the Learning Explosion. They are scattered bits of information and knowledge. Learning fragments can be found through many different sources such as social media sites, training workshops, video documentaries, online communities, blogs, books, and mobile apps.

*At a conference in Dallas, we asked the same two questions referenced above. A woman stood up in the audience and shared that she didn't know how to change the filter in her Dyson vacuum cleaner. To find her answer, she didn't call the vacuum store. She didn't pull out her owner's manual—either because she didn't have one, or it was lost or tossed. She went to the manufacturer's website first, but she couldn't find the exact answer to her specific question. She then went to a community site where other people had the same problem. There, she was able to quickly learn what she needed to know in order to accomplish her task. If she needed more help, she could have easily located tens of thousands of other learning fragments in the form of videos, documents, or blog posts.*

I'm sure she could have gone to the store where she purchased her vacuum to find a salesperson who could answer her question. But why? She could find learning fragments faster, easier, and cheaper than ever before without leaving her home, through her smartphone, computer, or tablet.

*Another friend of ours told us how she dropped her iPhone, cracking the screen. Instead of giving in and buying a brand-new phone, she turned to one of her learning-fragment sources, YouTube, for the answer. There she found step-by-step video instructions on how to replace the cracked screen with a new screen, which she bought for a mere $20.*

Think about this fundamental change in the way people gain their knowledge. Learners no longer have to travel to a specific training destination to find information. They can simply turn on their phone to instantly find learning fragments or turn on their computer and attend a virtual classroom. We agree that these examples may seem simplistic. But that is the point. We can learn almost anything—right now!

## Sharing Your Learning Fragments

The ability to share learning fragments with friends or colleagues is one of their greatest attributes. The act of sharing something we like or have learned strengthens the learning experience that has just taken place and provides additional opportunities for reinforcement and even deeper learning.

> *On a recent business trip, we found ourselves in the historic town of Princeton, New Jersey. After getting off the airplane and into our rental car, a number of interesting things happened. First, Treion got out his iPhone and opened the Tripit[13] application that not only gave detailed information about the hotel and the surrounding city, but also linked to his phone's map application, providing step-by-step directions to the hotel. After checking in at the hotel, we decided to go into downtown Princeton to have dinner. So Matt opened up the Urbanspoon[14] application on his iPhone and shared the ratings and recommendations for several restaurants with Treion (recommendations from complete strangers, mind you). We selected a highly rated Italian restaurant named Teresa Caffe.[15] While eating, Treion felt compelled to "check in" to the restaurant via his Foursquare[16] application—again, with the hope that complete strangers would benefit by what he was saying. Matt, inspired by the history of Princeton, searched Wikipedia on his phone and shared the town's history with Treion. You get the idea. We were finding new learning fragments for relevant information.*

We know we should have probably put the phones away and had a normal conversation between colleagues. For the record, this extreme example is not typical. However, with so many learning fragments available to us through our smartphones and computers, we tend to turn to them for relevant information often.

The sharing of learning fragments has become so commonplace and easy, we are all participating in some way or another. This is the magic of the Learning Explosion. Experts and novices around the world are sharing learning fragments via blogs, websites, Twitter, tools, wikis, and many other learning-fragment sources.

To help illustrate this concept of learning-fragment sharing, we have included learning fragments throughout the book. We have also created several dynamic resource sites for you to discover new learning fragments (see the table on the next page). We encourage you to take advantage of them, find your own, and share them with others.

### The Learning-Fragment Game

The next time you are with a group of friends or students, play the Learning-Fragment Game.

1. Pick a topic (abstract or relevant).

2. Give everyone 3 minutes to go online, using whatever device they have, to learn about the subject.

3. Have everyone report what they learned and which learning fragments they used to find the information.

4. Share these learning fragments and their locations.

You'll be amazed at the wide variety of places people go to find information. You'll also be amazed at how much you will learn.

## The Learning Explosion Resource Sites

| Resource | Description |
|---|---|
| Twitter.com | Twitter can be an effective learning tool. We use it as a means of discovering and sharing learning fragments. twitter.com/learningexplosn |
| Twitter Hashtag | Whenever you discover a new learning fragment, just add #LFRAG to your tweet. This way #LFRAG becomes an online location for sharing learning fragments with each other. Even if you are not an active tweeter, you can still go to twitter.com and search #LFRAG to view what others are discovering. |
| Blog | Read our blog posts as we look at the future of learning, interesting trends, and relevant learning news. thelearningexplosion.com |
| Book Website | Access some of the Learning Explosion Action Plans, plus you can see our rolling Twitter feed at franklincovey.com/thelearningexplosion. |
| Facebook | If Facebook is your social-media preference, then like "The Learning Explosion" and follow us there. |
| LinkedIn | To engage Matt and Treion in conversation, please connect with us on LinkedIn.com. linkedin.com/in/mattmurdoch linkedin.com/in/treionmuller |

## Organizing Your Learning Fragments

Having a convenient way to collect and aggregate relevant learning fragments in one place is imperative for the effective harnessing of the Learning Explosion. There are so many ways for you to collect and organize your learning-fragment sources, that to try and list them all would be futile. However, we would like to introduce you to some of our most favorite.

## Learning-Fragment Organizers

### BOOKMARKS

Probably the most basic and widespread example of aggregating learning-fragment sources is the "bookmarks" function found on every Internet browser—even on mobile devices. It can be used to organize and categorize websites to meet your personal learning needs.

### MOBILE PHONE FOLDERS

In the Princeton example, the iPhone became the tool we used to organize our learning-fragment sources. With many mobile phones, you can organize your apps into relevant folders.

### GENIEO.COM[17]

Based on your specific individual interests, Genieo automatically retrieves and filters information from across the Web. It displays them on a personal homepage created exclusively for you.

### FEEDLY.COM[18]

Organize your favorite sources into a magazine-like homepage.

### FLIPBOARD (FOR IPAD)[19]

Provides a customizable interface that receives RSS feeds from industry sites and connects to social media sites.

## The Next Best Thing Is Now!

But what do the Learning Explosion and learning fragments have to do with moving your corporate learning to the virtual classroom? Everything!

The Learning Explosion is happening, whether we like it or not. Even before we introduced the concept of the Learning Explosion in this book, we're confident most people were already aware of the notion.

We have discovered that the general population and pundits alike are already speculating about what the next best learning gadget, tool, application, or invention will be.

Just recently, we heard a keynote speaker ask the audience how they thought we would be learning in five years. We looked at each other and both said, "Who cares about five years?" The next best thing is now! And thanks to the Learning Explosion, we have the next best learning innovations flowing to us daily. Don't misunderstand us. We expect technology to continue to leap forward, but we enjoy living in it and experiencing it as it grows. But if you keep looking forward 5 or 10 years, you're going to miss what's happening today.

**YOUR VIRTUAL CLASSROOM**

The exciting challenge we have now is finding new and creative ways of organizing learning fragments, and experimenting with new ways to include them in our virtual classrooms and other learning platforms. This is how you apply the new learning mind-set. Only with this foundational mind-set in place are we sufficiently prepared to incorporate the new rule-set.

## Rule [rool] -noun

A principle or regulation governing conduct, action, procedure, arrangement, etc.[20]

We suggest there are nine rules for creating high-quality and effective virtual classrooms:

The Rule of Continual Change

The Rule of Knowledge Transfer

The Rule of Learning Circuitry

The Rule of Overcoming Bias

The Rule of Virtual Accountability

The Rule of Personal Practice

The Rule of Thumbs Up

The Rule of Global Positioning

The Rule of Sustained Orbit

## Learning Explosion Action Plan

### YOUR LEARNING FRAGMENTS

Do a quick inventory of your current learning fragments by writing down the sources you frequently use.

| Learning-Fragment Source | Description |
|---|---|
| *Example: YouTube* | *Video-based learning* |
| | |
| | |
| | |
| | |
| | |
| | |
| | |
| | |
| | |
| | |
| | |
| | |
| | |
| | |
| | |
| | |
| | |
| | |
| | |
| | |
| | |

# The
# New
# Rule-Set

# CHAPTER 3

# The Rule of Continual Change

**TWITTER SUMMARY ≤ 140 CHARACTERS**

The way people learn will always change. If you wish to embrace the Learning Explosion, you must change as well.

We introduce this rule first, because it is the only one that will always be relevant yet never change.

*We recently heard an astonishing story from Curtis Morley, a colleague of ours who teaches at a respected university.*

*While presenting to a group of master's-level students about technology, he mentioned something about an email he had received when, from the middle of the auditorium, a student shouted out, "Email is for old people!"*

*This comment caught him off guard. He stopped his presentation and asked who made this bold statement. The audience was large enough and the room lights were dimmed low enough that he couldn't pick the student out himself. After some cajoling by his peers, a lone hand was raised and the once-brazen student admitted to the outburst.*

*Curtis asked the student what he meant by "email is for old people." The student went on to explain that no one uses email anymore, except when required by professors to check grades. The other students seemed to affirm this as well. Being so interested in learning more, Curtis completely abandoned his prepared presentation and started questioning the group. The following dialogue is taken directly from his blog.[21]*

*"So who uses email on regular basis?"*

*Less than a fourth of the hands went up.*

*"How do you get hold of one another?"*

*"We text, Twitter, or Facebook," they said. "Email is so slow. We want to get hold of our friends instantly."*

*"How many of you will text first instead of calling on the phone?"*

*Almost all hands were raised.*

*"How do you communicate anything substantial [on Twitter] with only 140 characters?"*

*"You only need 140 characters to say what you need to say," someone replied.*

*"Facebook is for bigger stuff and pictures. And if you really need to write something big, you just post it to your blog. I have an RSS feed of all my friends' blogs," commented another student.*

Like Curtis, we were very surprised to learn how much communication had changed. These same master's-level students are soon going to be working in organizations where email is a staple of corporate life.

While this small sample of students—in one auditorium, at one university—may not represent the majority of learners out there, one thing is for certain: things are definitely changing.

Learning has been in a state of change forever—slowly evolving. But with the current explosion, learning is anything but slow. It is rapid. Instant. Continuously changing. Morphing. Upgrading.

**Evolution** [ev-uh-loo-shuh] -noun
A process of continuous change from a lower, simpler, or worse to a higher, more complex, or better state.[22]

Maybe email will not suffer the same fate as other learning tools of the past—like the typewriter, carbon paper, and overhead projector—but change it will.

Along these lines of change, there are places online where you can experience lectures and workshops from highly qualified faculty and respected business leaders. Academic Earth[23] is one such place. It was founded with the goal of giving everyone on earth access to a world-class education. Do we believe that the education you will get from Academic Earth—even with Harvard Faculty—matches the experience of attending courses on the Harvard campus? No, not yet. But at the advancement of the Learning Explosion, it eventually will.

Virtual classrooms are fast becoming one of these online tools of choice. For example, at General Motors, they understand how learning is changing, and have already initiated a large-scale transition to virtual classrooms.

**Real-World Example**

## GENERAL MOTORS—FROM SATELLITES TO VIRTUAL CLASSROOMS

Launched as part of a blended-learning solution at more than 5,000 GM dealerships in North America, GM partnered with Dallas-based Raytheon Professional Services LLC (RPS) to build virtual-classroom training that replaced a satellite-based distance-learning system that has helped train dealer employees for over a decade. John Palmer, manager of GM Learning, reports that the solution is winning over employees and management alike with its broad functionality, ease of operation, and cost-saving features. Some 200,000 employees in North America alone will rely on the system, as well as thousands more in other countries.

"I actually believe it's a better delivery method than having an instructor in the room," says Palmer. He calls virtual-classroom training an invaluable tool for reaching the widely dispersed population of GM dealer employees. GM is rolling out its enhanced distance-learning capabilities worldwide with the help of Raytheon Professional Services. A division of defense-and-aerospace giant Raytheon Company, RPS has helped provide training at GM dealerships throughout North America, Europe, and other global locations for over a decade.

Our legacy satellite-learning system was state of the art in its time, but virtual-classroom training is a far superior technology," Palmer told the group. He said GM has selected Adobe® Connect™ as its tool. It enables users to create, deploy, and manage live virtual classrooms while operating seamlessly within a powerful learning-management system developed internally by Raytheon.

Yet, as valuable as virtual classrooms and other training tools have become in today's learning landscape, their benefits are only realized when they are properly supported by sound management. GM points out that the entire training program is supported by the people, processes, and governance necessary to ensure quality and success.[24]

This move to the virtual classroom is no anomaly. Companies like GM must anticipate change, research it, and ultimately embrace it in order to survive the constant explosion of ideas, innovations, and knowledge.

## Learning Explosion Action Plan

**THE RULE OF CONTINUAL CHANGE**

Take a moment to answer the following questions:

1. How has the delivery of training changed in your organization over the past five years?

_____

_____

2. How are you preparing for future changes in learning delivery?

_____

_____

3. If there is one thing you could change about how training is being delivered, what would it be?

_____

_____

4. Ask five people in your organization how they prefer to *communicate*.

   a. Phone

   b. Email

   c. Text

   d. Social Media

   e. Other

5. Ask those same five people how they prefer to *learn*. (Do not provide any suggestions so that you do not influence their answers. Just listen and learn.)

_____

_____

_____

_____

.

# CHAPTER 4

# The Rule of Knowledge Transfer

**TWITTER SUMMARY ≤ 140 CHARACTERS**

Transitioning from instructor-led training to virtual classrooms requires a new approach to content, length, instructional design, & delivery.

*Just a couple of years ago, we worked with a disgruntled client who was not happy about having to make the switch from his comfort zone—the traditional classroom—to what he referred to as the ugly stepsister: the virtual classroom. His case against this new delivery channel was sound. For starters, there just wasn't enough time to teach all he had to teach in the suggested shorter time frame. How was he going to involve his audience, whom he couldn't see, and who he couldn't even tell were listening? Then there was the issue of modifying his well-crafted exercises to work in the virtual classroom. And how could he, or anyone for that matter, effectively teach while talking to a computer screen? As you can tell, he was pretty adamant that this new form of delivery would not work for him.*

*Just a few months later, this same client became one of the biggest champions of virtual classrooms, choosing it over traditional face-to-face training.*

What changed in such a short period of time? The answer can be found in the Rule of Knowledge Transfer.

## Knowledge transfer [nol-ij trans-fur] -noun

Knowledge transfer is the act or process of transferring information—in this case, from the traditional classroom to the new virtual classroom.

The reason this client was successful in making the move from one delivery channel to another was because he was willing to change his behavior with regard to four training approaches: content, length, instructional design, and delivery.

We will start by introducing you to these four new approaches in this chapter but will also go into more detail in future chapters.

### 1. Content

The first approach that needs to change is the amount of content used. Don't try to force the same amount of content you usually teach in insuctor-led training (ILT) programs into your virtual classrooms. Just because you have eight hours worth of face-to-face training content doesn't mean you have eight hours worth of virtual training content. There is a lot more learners can assimilate when they are physically present, compared to what they can assimilate when they are only present virtually.

Faced with these limitations and challenges, you can still effectively transfer your ILT content to the virtual classroom using two proven methods: summarizing and chunking.

## Instructor-led training [in-struhk-ter led trey-ning] -noun

ILT usually refers to traditional classroom training, in which an instructor teaches a course to a room of learners. The term is used synonymously with on-site training and classroom training.[25]

> **Real-World Example**
>
> ### THE 7 HABITS OF HIGHLY EFFECTIVE PEOPLE® FOR ASSOCIATES WORKSHOP
>
>
>
> This FranklinCovey ILT workshop can be delivered in several ways: in one-day, two half-day, or four 2-hour sessions. It covers the principles from Stephen R. Covey's best-selling business book *The 7 Habits of Highly Effective People*. The workshop has been designed and developed with best-practice instructional design in mind, including frequent and varied interaction, reinforcement, and engaging exercises.
>
> We will reference back to this workshop frequently in this chapter. To understand how we changed our approach in regard to content, we will use this simplified course outline:
>
> - Introduction
> - Habit 1: Be Proactive®
> - Habit 2: Begin With the End in Mind®
> - Habit 3: Put First Things First®
> - Habit 4: Think Win-Win®
> - Habit 5: Seek First to Understand, Then to Be Understood®
> - Habit 6: Synergize®
> - Habit 7: Sharpen the Saw®

### *Summarizing*

As the name implies, you simply provide a shorter virtual-classroom version of the full ILT course. This well-established instructional approach works just as effectively in the virtual classroom as it does in traditional ILT. The key with this approach is to focus on the core principles, skills, and/or techniques you want your learners to adopt, and only include that content in your virtual classroom. It will be very hard to part with all of the excess content, stories, and exercises you have been refining for years, but this you must do to apply this knowledge-transfer approach.

---

**Real-World Example**

**SUMMARIZING**

In the summarizing approach, we took the seven hours worth of content from the ILT workshop and divided it into two 90-minute virtual classrooms we named *The 7 Habits Jump Start Series*. If you are doing the math with us, that means we only used three hours of a seven-hour workshop. We trimmed back the excess content, adapted the exercises, and created two "summary" webinars.

The content was divided as follows:

- The 7 Habits Jump Start Series: Habits 1–3 (which includes the Introduction)

- The 7 Habits Jump Start Series: Habits 4–7

---

### Chunking

If you do not wish to part with all of your material, then you should break that content up into separate virtual classroom "chunks" or sessions. With this option, you end up keeping much more of the original content and learners simply attend multiple sessions. With the chunking approach, you may also consider teaching your virtual-classroom sessions over a couple of days or even weeks. Don't feel like you need to try and cram them all in one day. Spacing your events apart allows you to build more of a blended-learning experience with assignments, exercises, and other asynchronous learning modules built in between.

**Real-World Example**

**CHUNKING**

For the chunking approach, the intent was to include as much of the seven-hours worth of content as possible. To do so, we created *The 7 Habits Associates Full-Day Webinar*. While we only ended up with 4.5 hours of instruction, we broke up the training so that it could be experienced in one day or divided up over several days.

- Introduction and Habit 1 (90-minute webinar)
- Break (1 hour)
- Habits 2, 3, 4 (90-minute webinar)
- Break (1 hour)
- Habits 5, 6, 7 (90-minute webinar)

## 2. Length

The second approach you should consider is the length of your virtual classroom. Some organizations keep their virtual classrooms as short as 20 minutes. Others have successfully facilitated three or four sessions of up to three-hours each, with breaks in between—breaks that range from an hour to days or even weeks. Some people build day-long experiences that are broken up into 90-minute chunks.

Our personal experience has shown that anything longer than two hours per session is too long, even with frequent and a varied interaction. We believe that 90- to 120-minute sessions are an ideal length for a virtual classroom experience. It allows you enough time to teach three or four main points and is short enough to keep people engaged.

We recognize that every situation is different. You should test various combinations and options yourself until you find the perfect amount of content and length for your virtual classroom.

It is important to note that there is a point of diminishing returns with how much your learner can absorb in a single online session. As you teach your sessions, you'll get a sense for when this point is reached and you'll be able to modify your delivery as needed. While you may be familiar with this concept in a traditional classroom, the ability for you to sense when to move on and adapt your teaching is more difficult to detect in a virtual classroom, mainly because it is a new mode of delivery, but also because you simply cannot see your learners. Developing an accurate sense of time and rhythm in the virtual space will take time and practice. Don't force it. The more time you spend in your virtual classroom interacting with your learners, the more acute your senses will become.

A major benefit of virtual classrooms is that online exercises and activities generally take less time to complete. For example, a small-group activity, where you divide your audience into groups of four and have them work on a problem together, can be facilitated with four chat pods or a whiteboard tool in a virtual classroom. With the instructor discussing comments and asking for elaboration, you can end up with the same results but in less time.

## Real-World Example

### TIME AND DESIGN COMPARISON

To illustrate how we changed our instructional-design approach in regard to length, we'll use sections from the one-day workshop *The 7 Habits of Highly Effective People for Associates*. This table shows how we adapted it to one of our 90-minute virtual-classroom offerings.

| ILT Workshop | Virtual Classroom |
|---|---|
| **The Time Matrix** *(Approximate length of activity: 10 minutes)* | **The Time Matrix** *(Approximate length of activity: 5 minutes)* |
| Create four flip charts labeled with a different quadrant (I, II, III, IV). | Create four chat pods labeled with a different quadrant (I, II, III, IV). |
| Draw three columns in each flip chart, one on the left labeled "Activities," one in the middle labeled "Feelings," and one on the right labeled "Long-Term Impact." | 1. Chat: Answer the question for each quadrant in the chat pods: "What would be the long-term results if you spent MOST of your time in each quadrant?" Imagine that these chat pods are four flip charts around the room. Add your thoughts to each one. |
| Divide participants into four groups and assign each group to a flip chart. | |
| 1. State: Assume you live in your assigned quadrant. In the first column, write down what you would spend the majority of your time doing. In the second column, write down how spending the majority of your time in this quadrant would make you feel. In the third column, write down what the long-term impact would be of spending your time there. | 2. Debrief the chat-pod responses.<br><br>3. Ask: If you could spend the majority of your time in one quadrant, which one would you choose? Why? |
| 2. Ask: If you could spend the majority of your time in one quadrant, which one would you choose? Why? | |

### 3. Instructional Design

Please note: [What works in the traditional classroom may not work online.] We could have very easily taken our well-balanced interactive ILT, thrown it into a virtual-classroom platform, and shared PowerPoint slide after PowerPoint slide while lecturing our poor audience to sleep. This point may seem obvious, but unfortunately, this is how much of today's online synchronous learning is taking place.

When you begin building your new virtual-classroom experience, think about who your virtual learners are. They are most likely sitting at their desk surrounded by numerous other potential distractions like email, the Web, co-workers, background noise, cell and work phones, bosses, their job responsibilities, and much more. In other words, they are just looking for an opportunity to leave your online lecture to update their Facebook status with something like "I would rather crawl across a field of broken glass than attend this boring webinar."

So knowing that you have to win the battle of distraction, you will need to build a virtual experience with frequent interaction and engagement. We share proven behaviors and practices on how to do this throughout the book.

## Real-World Example

### INSTRUCTIONAL-DESIGN COMPARISON

Review the sections from the original one-day workshop and the virtual-classroom offerings, and compare the instructional-design differences.

| ILT Workshop | Virtual Classroom |
|---|---|
| **Example 1: Maturity Continuum Outline** *(Approximate length of activity: 10 minutes)* | **Example 1: Maturity Continuum Outline** *(Approximate length of activity: 5 minutes)* |
| 1. Show Slide 10, "Maturity Continuum." | 1. Show Slide 10, "Maturity Continuum." |
| 2. State: Turn to page 4 in your participant guide. This model is known as the Maturity Continuum. It shows how all of the habits build on each other to reach higher and higher levels of maturity. | 2. State: Turn to page 4 in your participant guide. This model is known as the Maturity Continuum. It shows how all of the habits build on each other to reach higher and higher levels of maturity. |
| The 7 Habits form the Maturity Continuum, leading you on the path to interdependence. You must first be effective at leading your own life (the Private Victory) before you can successfully work with others (the Public Victory). | The 7 Habits form the Maturity Continuum, leading you on the path to interdependence. You must first be effective at leading your own life (the Private Victory) before you can successfully work with others (the Public Victory). |
| 3. Team Activity: Move from dependence to interdependence. In your teams, identify the behaviors of people at work who fall within your assigned level of maturity. For example, people who are dependent often rely on others or on their own title to feel validated. | 3. Chat-Pod Activity: Move from dependence to interdependence. In the chat pods, identify the behaviors of people at work who fall within each level of maturity. For example, people who are dependent often rely on others or on their own title to feel validated. |
| After you have identified specific behaviors, discuss the effectiveness or ineffectiveness of working with these individuals. | Debrief responses, pointing out the effectiveness and ineffectiveness of working with these individuals. |

## Real-World Example

### INSTRUCTIONAL-DESIGN COMPARISON

Review the sections from the original one-day workshop and the virtual-classroom offerings, and compare the instructional-design differences.

| ILT Workshop | Virtual Classroom |
|---|---|
| **Example 2: Reactive/ Proactive Exercise** *(Approximate length of activity: 5 minutes)* | **Example 2: Reactive/ Proactive Exercise** *(Approximate length of activity: 5 minutes)* |
| 1. State: Let's look at the impact of proactive versus reactive behavior. | 1. State: Let's look at the impact of proactive versus reactive behavior. |
| I'm going to read several statements. As a group, determine if the statement is proactive or reactive. | 2. Poll Pod: Ask participants to answer each poll question as you read it. |
| • Someone cuts you off in traffic, so you gesture inappropriately. | • Someone cuts you off in traffic, so you gesture inappropriately. |
| • You feel like you are being scheduled for too many long shifts at work. Instead of complaining to your co-workers, you talk to your manager calmly about the issue. | • You feel like you are being scheduled for too many long shifts at work. Instead of complaining to your co-workers, you talk to your manager calmly about the issue. |
| • A customer complains for the third time in a week about the same thing. You tell him to gripe to somebody else because there's nothing you can do about it, or get a new complaint. | • A customer complains for the third time in a week about the same thing. You tell him to gripe to somebody else because there's nothing you can do about it, or get a new complaint. |
| • Your manager criticizes your attitude in front of your peers. You say, "I can't help it—that's the way I was raised," and blow it off. | • Your manager criticizes your attitude in front of your peers. You say, "I can't help it—that's the way I was raised," and blow it off. |

The lesson we can learn from this small comparison is that while transferring ILT to a virtual classroom requires a lot of upfront review and time, it often demands less tweaking than you may think. However, to successfully apply this Rule of Knowledge Transfer to instructional design, it's helpful to have a proven methodology or process you can follow.

## The SOLID Process

After years of designing and developing highly interactive virtual classrooms, we believe we have a sound instructional-design knowledge-transfer process. We call this process Simple Online-Learning Instructional Design, or the SOLID Process. SOLID is an introductory 10-step process that incorporates:

- Our simplicity approach to learning.

- Best practices from traditional and virtual instructional-design theory.

- Practices and procedures we have personally experienced and tested.

This process assumes you already have a well-designed ILT workshop from which to start and you have a fundamental knowledge of your chosen virtual-classroom platform. Keep in mind that creating a completely new virtual classroom from scratch requires some additional analysis, design, and evaluation not covered in SOLID.

## The SOLID Process

Step 1.     Identify the ILT you wish to transfer to a virtual classroom.

Step 2.     Pinpoint what current ILT course materials you already have. (Example: outlines, PowerPoint slide deck, participant guide, facilitator guide, course videos, etc.)

Step 3.     Select the content approach you plan on using: summarizing or chunking.

Step 4.     List the virtual-classroom tools you have on your chosen platform. (Example: chat, polls, whiteboard, breakout functionality, assessments, emoticons, screen sharing, etc.)

Step 5.     Develop your virtual-classroom outline with your platform tools, your content approach, and instructional-design best practices in mind.

Step 6.     Adapt the current ILT course materials to the needs of your virtual classroom.

Step 7.     Review your prototype with the content subject-matter expert (SME) and make appropriate changes.

Step 8.     Test with end users.

Step 9.     Receive and apply feedback.

Step 10.   Repeat testing and feedback steps until you feel it is ready for launch.

The SOLID process may seem like a major oversimplification of some major learning theories and concepts. For example, the principle of feedback has several theories and dozens of books by well-known thought leaders, yet we have taken this large body of work and simplified it down to one step in the SOLID process. We have done the same with other steps in the process.

So while our SOLID process may seem like a oversimplification, it is in reality the result of years of complex testing, trial, and error, each step representing a personalized solution to our unique set of challenges.

We share our SOLID process with you in hope that you will use it as a guide in which to build your own process. Consider your organizational needs, challenges, culture, and existing systems as you craft and weave your very own virtual-classroom instructional-design process. Remember to take advantage of the many learning fragments available to you, give proper attribution to the sources you use, and share your findings with your fellow Learning Explosion colleagues.

**Learning Fragment**

**LINKEDIN.COM, INSTRUCTIONAL DESIGN & E-LEARNING PROFESSIONALS' GROUP[26]**
Join this group to ask questions and learn from community members about instructional-design best practices.

## 4. Delivery

The number-one concern we hear from new virtual-classroom instructors is how to engage learners. The guidance we give these instructors is to approach delivery from two separate areas of emphasis: virtual learning environment and delivery technique.

### *Virtual Learning Environment*

While there are distinct differences between ILT and virtual classrooms, there are also many similarities, like preparing your physical learning environment. In your ILT classroom, you take time to set up the projector, flip charts, tables, and chairs. Some of you also check the temperature of the training room and even provide "toys" for people to use during the training.

Since this same principle applies to the virtual classroom, you should pay just as much attention to getting your virtual learning environment ready for the instructor and learners. With the help of Dave Green, one of FranklinCovey's expert delivery consultants, we have come up with some proven ways you can prepare for a positive virtual learning environment.

Before we look at these proven methods, it is important to understand that there are some realities about your learners' physical environment that you just can't control. Don't let these distractions frazzle you. You just have to go with it. Some distractions may include:

- Speaker-phone feedback
- Groups chatting and talking
- People keyboarding loudly

- Other phones ringing
- People walking in and talking
- Low cube walls and high-noise area

### Proven Methods of Preparing Your Virtual Learning Environment

Learner Preparation

- Before attending the event, check to see that you have all the right equipment and network connection.
- Print out any necessary materials.
- Warn your co-workers and boss beforehand that you will be busy during that time.
- Place a "Do Not Disturb" sign on your door (or somewhere conspicuous in your cubicle).
- Turn your cell phone off, not just on vibrate.
- Eliminate all sources of noise or interruptions.
- Shut down all other programs on your computer—especially email.
- Have a bottle of water and a snack on hand.
- Visit the restroom beforehand.

Instructor Preparation

- Apply all of the same practices you are asking your learners to follow.
- Since your computer is your training room, take precautionary steps to ensure that it is functioning properly.

- If you facilitate many virtual-classroom events, it's advisable to have a second computer as a backup. While this may seem extreme, the first time your computer dies, you will thank us.

- The same could be said of your network connection. A higher-end, more reliable connection is always safer and faster than the opposite, plus your learners will thank you for a better-quality experience.

- Never facilitate a virtual-classroom event from a hotel room unless you have tested the reliability of the connection. Most hotels claim to have a good connection, but very few can back up that statement.

- Warm up your voice and get energized. Our friend Dave actually puts on his favorite rock song and sings along to it before going "on stage."

### Delivery Technique

With virtual classrooms, you engage your learners differently than you would in a typical ILT session. In some cases, you have the opportunity of engaging them even more. In this section, we introduce you to some basic delivery starter tips you can use to prepare for your virtual-classroom event. We have also included a "Virtual-Classroom Delivery Checklist" at the end of this chapter. In addition to these delivery resources, we go into more detail in Chapter 7: The Rule of Virtual Accountability on how to engage your learners.

As you start experiencing the Rule of Knowledge Transfer, you may find that great ILT instructors do not always make great virtual instructors. The main reasons for this can be illustrated in the following example.

## Real-World Example

### DELIVERY DON'TS

Manny [pseudonym] has been a facilitator of live, in-person training with the same company for 15 years. He is a good facilitator. He is a subject-matter expert on all of his company's intellectual property and has trained people in every department—from the front line to the executive suite. He has been asked by the vice-president of HR to start teaching the same content in virtual classrooms to save money and reach more employees. Manny reluctantly agrees. He's told not to worry, because all he has to do is show up and do what he has always done. Everything else has been taken care of.

The day arrives, and Manny follows the instructions he received in an email on how to get into his new classroom. He is not overly concerned because he has a "techie" to run the newfangled Web-classroom "thingy." However, he soon realizes that this new "thingy" has its own challenges. Manny cannot see his learners or their body language, and they seem mighty quiet. He has always prided himself in being able to "read" his audience, but not anymore. He soon gets nervous and just keeps on talking. Before long, he has effectively sped through everything he was asked to teach. What would usually take him half a day in a live classroom has lasted less than an hour.

Feeling good about surviving his first virtual classroom, Manny ends the experience by opening it up for Q&A. But only a few people have stayed on, and they are too exhausted and confused to ask meaningful questions. He gets very poor feedback scores for the first time in his life. Manny blames the virtual-classroom technology for the failure.

While Manny was set up to fail by being told to just show up and do what he has always done, he should have given more thought about the technology he was going to use and taken much more time to prepare.

Like Manny, sometimes we just need a little guidance around what we should and should not do. So here are some basic tips on the most common dos and don'ts of virtual classrooms:

## Delivery Starter Tips

| Delivery Don'ts | Delivery Dos |
|---|---|
| • Lecture your audience. | • Plan for frequent interactivity. |
| • Beat the same old PowerPoint drum. | • Use various forms of visuals throughout. |
| • Wing it. | • Practice adequately. |
| • Only allow questions at the end. | • Involve participants verbally throughout. |
| • Expect to do things the same way. | • Adapt instruction and exercises. |
| • Do it the same every time. | • Get feedback every time, listen, and apply feedback. |
| • Give participants nothing to do. | • Provide participant materials/ handouts. |
| • Rely on someone else solely to "drive" the platform. | • Know your delivery-platform tools. |

Unlike Manny in the example we used earlier, great instructors of the new virtual-classroom era don't rely solely on their knowledge of the content to get them through; they take the time to adapt what they teach and how they deliver it. They understand that a new delivery channel requires a new skill-set. And they understand that it requires time and practice to master the virtual classroom.

To successfully transfer your corporate classroom online requires you to change your approach when it comes to what content to include, how long your sessions should be, how best to teach that content, and how to effectively deliver that content. Just understanding that a virtual classroom requires these different approaches is great start.

## Learning Explosion Action Plan

### THE RULE OF KNOWLEDGE TRANSFER

### SOLID PROCESS CHECKLIST

Use these SOLID 10 steps to create your next virtual classroom.

Step 1.  Identify the ILT you wish to transfer to a virtual classroom.

○ Completed

Step 2.  Pinpoint what current ILT course materials you already have.

○ Outline

○ PowerPoint® slide deck

○ Participant guide

○ Facilitator guide

○ Course videos

○ Other

Step 3.  Select the content approach you plan on using.

○ Summarizing

○ Chunking

Step 4.  Mark the virtual-classroom tools you have on your chosen platform.

○ Chat

○ Polling

○ Whiteboard

○ Breakout functionality

○ Assessments

○ Emoticons

○ Screen sharing

○ Video

○ Web links

○ File sharing

○ Other

## Learning Explosion Action Plan

# THE RULE OF KNOWLEDGE TRANSFER
# SOLID PROCESS CHECKLIST (CONT.)

Step 5. Develop your virtual-classroom outline with these three things in mind:
- ○ Virtual-classroom platform tools
- ○ Summarizing or chunking approach
- ○ Instructional-design best practices

Step 6. Adapt the current ILT course materials to the needs of your virtual classroom.
- ○ PowerPoint® slide deck
- ○ Participant guide
- ○ Facilitator guide
- ○ Course videos
- ○ Other

Step 7. Review your prototype with the content subject-matter expert (SME) and make appropriate changes.
- ○ Review completed

Step 8. Test with end users.
- ○ Testing completed

Step 9. Receive feedback.
- ○ Feedback completed

Step 10. Repeat testing and feedback steps until you get it right.
- ○ Completed

## Learning Explosion Action Plan

**VIRTUAL-CLASSROOM DELIVERY CHECKLIST**

### TWO WEEKS BEFORE THE EVENT

- ◯ Review the content and all of the materials.
- ◯ Send out the event invitations with the Virtual Learning Environment recommendations.
- ◯ Test all technical components of your virtual-classroom platform with your IT team.
- ◯ Practice teaching with other people if possible.

### THE DAY OF THE EVENT

- ◯ Double-check your network connection.
- ◯ Close down all other applications and programs on your computer.
- ◯ Eliminate all sources of noise or interruptions.
- ◯ Place a "Do Not Disturb" sign on your door.
- ◯ Warm up your voice and get energized.

### 30–60 MINUTES PRIOR TO THE EVENT

- ◯ Boot your computer up and get online.
- ◯ Close your door and place your phones on forward.
- ◯ Eat and drink something for energy.
- ◯ Visit the restroom.

### 10–30 MINUTES PRIOR TO THE EVENT

- ◯ Log on to your virtual classroom and display your welcome screen.
- ◯ Get your training guide ready.
- ◯ Place your headset on.

## Learning Explosion Action Plan

**VIRTUAL-CLASSROOM DELIVERY
CHECKLIST (CONT.)**

**0–10 MINUTES PRIOR TO THE EVENT**

| | |
|---|---|
| ○ | Start welcoming participants. |
| ○ | Go over virtual-classroom dos and don'ts. |

**NOTES**

What if we provided
SGs for LL?

On Message Board
webmail?

Print or open.

# CHAPTER 5

# The Rule of Learning Circuitry

**TWITTER SUMMARY ≤ 140 CHARACTERS**

There are five steps to creating learning circuits within your organization. Use them to successfully launch and administer your virtual classrooms.

As we make the move to virtual classrooms, we must change traditional operational methods, processes, and systems. To ensure the success of your virtual-classroom program, you will need a strategic plan and the expertise of a core group of team members—team members with a new set of skills.

We personally experienced the Rule of Learning Circuitry when we created the first virtual-classroom initiative at FranklinCovey: LiveClicks™ webinar workshops. We had the daunting task of creating an online experience that would uphold the reputation of Franklin-Covey's world-class instructional design and corporate brand.

We started with just a small, dedicated team of individuals—namely, a business leader, an instructional designer, a marketing-and-operations manager, and an instructor. Although the core team was only made of four people, we also had a first-class internal support team and vendors who all contributed greatly to the success of the project. Without our IT team and operational support, all our efforts would have been fruitless.

Our initial goal was to take existing FranklinCovey content that was currently being delivered in traditional full-day or multiday workshops and create two-hour virtual training sessions. It took a while to get all of the wires soldered into place, but eventually, the learning circuitry started expanding throughout the company.

Fast-forward to today. We now have a very successful virtual-classroom solution that is growing substantially. How did we do it? It all comes down to learning circuitry.

### Learning circuitry [lur-ning sur-ki-tree] -noun

Learning circuitry is the way in which each group within your company or organization works together to help your training initiative succeed-- through connective operations, financial models, sales and marketing systems, and quality training and delivery.

Your organization most likely has some working systems and operations around your existing ILT methods—it's hardwired for that type of training and not for virtual classrooms. If your organization isn't already in the virtual-classroom business, it's probably not ready operationally or philosophically to support that business…yet. Play it safe by completing the following five steps to build the right learning circuitry throughout your organization.

### Step 1. Start With a Core Team

When you first begin the process of moving your training online, you may not want too many people on the project. Actually, in most cases, it's best to start with a small core team. Small teams can move fast and won't get bogged down in bureaucracy. You're going to need the flexibility to modify your circuitry quickly. Ideas will change; strategies will be modified. We guarantee it. So start small and nimble.

## Real-World Example

### TEAM FOCUS

As we looked at our new virtual-classroom initiative and where we needed to build circuitry, we asked each member of the team to answer just one question. You may want to do the same.

**Business Leader**
How can you finance the virtual-classroom initiative and position it with our executives?

**Instructional Designer**
How can you effectively transform our instructor-led training to a virtual-classroom format?

**Marketing/Operations**
If your target audience is internal: How can you get key individuals and departments on board with this new initiative?

If your target audience is external: How can you get our sales force to sell something new, and our internal departments to fulfill something they have never dealt with before?

**Instructor**
How will you learn more about virtual-classroom delivery so you can change your teaching style to fit this new format?

---

With every core-team member focusing on just one essential strategy, you'll be surprised at how quickly you make progress. But beware of overload. If you are not careful, your small team may take on too much too soon and get very little accomplished.

Another key to success is holding frequent meetings to share findings and report on progress. We've found it helpful to schedule daily morning meetings to keep us focused on our main goals. Plus, it offers us a chance to communicate as a team to resolve problems, celebrate successes, and ensure that we are keeping on task. The trick is to keep these meetings short—we only schedule 30 minutes. We've found that with regular communication, we don't need more than this to report in and get ready for the day.

So, what do you do if you are a single, solitary blinking light in the circuitry of your organization? You've got a great idea, but you're an island—there is nobody there to help you build the circuitry. The good news is that you can still make a difference. YOU can be the start of your organization's learning circuitry.

While it may take you longer to work through these steps and the other rules in this book, there are many who have been through the process already, like us, who can provide expert assistance. You can start with the next learning fragment.

### Learning Fragment

**THE ELEARNING GUILD WEBSITE**[27]
Join the guild and gain access to research papers, forums, publications, and thought leaders.

## Step 2. Think Big and Act Small

Create a vision of where you want your learning circuitry to go and then break down your vision into small, manageable pieces. With LiveClicks webinar workshops, we identified four initial stages and we've tried to hold as close to those as possible.

---

### Real-World Example

**LIVECLICKS' VISION**

1. Stage 1 was to simply produce more content taught by FranklinCovey instructors. We wanted to create 10 webinars on topics such as time management, leadership, and project management.

2. Stage 2 was to increase our distribution through external instructors. We needed to create a simple certification model for our clients, enabling them to teach our content through virtual classrooms.

3. Stage 3 was to open up our business model to our global offices and empower them to localize content and create virtual classrooms as needed.

4. Stage 4 was to utilize our instructional designers and processes to develop high-quality custom content for organizations needing virtual-classroom training.

---

We're now solidly moving into the fourth stage, which is pretty exciting, and we see more stages in the future. But had we not focused on completing the first stage—getting 10 webinars developed and on the market—we never would have gotten to where we are today.

Don't try to do everything at once. Stick to your phased approach and be patient. Take some time to learn and develop your skills and abilities, and before you know it, your vision will be reality.

### Learning Fragment

**BLOGRANK**[28]

BlogRank uses over 20 different factors to rank blogs in a variety of categories, including elearning. Take a minute to search BlogRank's "Top 25 elearningblogs" list for the one or two that provide you the best information.

## Step 3. Find Executive Champions

Finding executive sponsors for your project is most often a key indicator of success in building the right circuitry. They can help clear the path when needed and should also be willing to act as your champion.

The one language all executives understand is money! To get them on board, link your virtual-classroom project to a critical business initiative and let them know that it won't interfere with your job. If you believe in your idea, you'll find the time to do it.

When we started LiveClicks, we had other full-time jobs at the company. Matt helped run our corporate marketing and Treion designed and built other products. Had we not obtained the approval and support of a couple of key executives at first, LiveClicks would have continued to be seen as a "pet project." But we were able to effectively show them the vision, the stages we were going to take, and how it would provide crucial benefits to the organization and our clients.

A valuable asset to use in this step is a well-written and researched business plan. Take a look at some of the elements we used in ours.

## Real-World Example

### BUSINESS-PLAN OUTLINE

| | |
|---|---|
| Executive Summary | Explain exactly what you intend to achieve. |
| Short-Term Goals | What do you want to accomplish in the next 9 to 12 months? |
| Long-Term Goals | What do you intend to accomplish in the next 3 to 5 years? |
| Financial Calculations:<br>• Cost Savings<br>• Revenue- and Margin-Generated | Do you want to save money, make money, or both? Make this argument strong but realistic. |
| Project Costs | List items like the cost of the software, development costs, marketing and promotion expenses, and the cost of sales. |
| Marketing Plan | Describe how you are going to attract people to your virtual classrooms. |
| Competition | Provide details on competing products—it could even be your traditional ILT. |
| Threats and Assumptions | What could derail your project and what assumptions have you made? |
| Timing | Build a calendar showing key project milestones. |

## Step 4. Build It Right the First Time

Do the hard work up front. Make sure you've done your research, looked at the competition, and identified holes in your approach, then build your program according to your vision. You'll be able to make modifications along the way, but do your best to lay the right circuitry up front. For example, with LiveClicks, we originally started with an off-the-shelf, virtual-classroom platform, which didn't entirely fulfill our vision. We then began developing our own platform to meet our specifications. We were digging and building and chipping away at something we thought we needed. This failed too.

Eventually, we discovered another virtual-classroom platform that met most of our established criteria and could be tailored to meet additional needs. So with the help of a vendor, we built a customized interface to meet all of our requirements. Our technology foundation was built.

It's a simple concept, but often we rush into a decision and start building before an accurate plan is determined. Don't fall into this trap. You will save time, money, and your credibility if you simply identify your needs and then do your due diligence.

One very essential part of due diligence is involving your IT department as soon as possible. Probably the most undervalued group in any organization, this group of "tech geeks," as we like to call them, are key to the successful launch of your virtual-classroom initiative. They will know what it takes to build it right the first time.

## Real-World Example

### VIRTUAL-CLASSROOM PLATFORM CRITERIA

When we developed LiveClicks, we had some very specific criteria for our virtual classrooms. You should evaluate your needs and create a similar list of needed features.

- Ability to upload and play videos
- Ability to upload files (PowerPoint, images, audio)
- Screen sharing
- Chat feature
- Polling feature
- Full-screen recording
- Attendee listing/management
- Ability to create and replicate classroom templates
- Varying levels of access control between instructor and learner
- Ability to customize layout
- Ability for learners to download files
- Link to a satisfaction survey
- No software downloads for the end user (to reduce firewall issues)
- Security of our intellectual property
- Cost-effectiveness
- Scalable
- Certification system for instructors
- Global access through different portal systems
- Localizable in any language

## IT Team Worksheet

When moving over to a new virtual-classroom platform, work with your IT department to answer the following questions:

1. Has the virtual-classroom software been thoroughly tested on and verified compatible with the Internet browsers utilized by our company?

2. What, if any, browser plug-ins are required?

3. Is any other software required to be installed on the end-user computer or on corporate servers?

4. What, if any, browser settings need to be enabled/changed (JavaScript, cookies, ActiveX, etc)?

5. How are audio and video files accessed (progressive download, standard streaming, etc.)? Is this compatible with our network settings?

6. Does our corporate network have the necessary bandwidth required for viewing/listening to rich media files? Do remote offices or home-office users have the necessary bandwidth?

7. Do any corporate network settings need to be modified (Comm ports opened, firewall or other network security settings changed)?

8. Who does our IT department contact if we encounter technical problems or outages? What hours are they available? Types of support (email, chat, call)? What are the associated costs?

9. Does the selected virtual-classroom platform have a redundancy/disaster plan for the servers that host our corporate data?

10. Is an annual maintenance contract required? What are the associated costs?

11. Is there technical training available for our internal IT support staff?

12. If requested, can you provide technical references from your client base?

13. If necessary, how is ADA/508 compliance supported and handled?

## Step 5. Measure Your Progress and Tell Everyone About It

Finally, chart your progress. Make sure to track your forward momentum so that when the time comes to report on your status, you have data. Compare your data with traditional training so you can see how well you're doing against the norm. Watch key indicators such as the number of people you have trained, costs saved, and attendee feedback scores on course content and facilitator skills. (See the Rule of Thumbs Up beginning on page 127 for some ways to do this.)

**Real-World Example**

**BRAG SHEET**

Create a well-designed marketing brag sheet and share it with your organization. Some facts and figures you could share are:

- Total number of attendees
- Revenue
- Cost savings (example: cost to attend ILT vs. the cost to attend virtual classrooms)
- Spotlight story of specific projects
- Positive-feedback scores and comments

When the time is right and you have the right data, shout your successes. Let everyone know about this transformation in learning so that the momentum keeps growing.

Building your learning circuitry is not going to be quick or easy. But the time you take to create learning circuitry within your organization will not only help you move your corporate learning online, but also help you gain more credibility and prominence in your organization.

## Learning Explosion Action Plan

### THE RULE OF LEARNING CIRCUITRY
Take a moment to answer the following questions:

1. Who is part of your virtual-classroom core team? Or who should be on the team?

2. What is your "big idea" or vision for online learning at your organization?

3. What training would be the best and easiest to start with?

4. Who on your executive team is, or can become, a champion for online learning?

5. Do you have a business plan you can present to your executive champion?

6. Have you involved your IT team?

7. What will you do to find out what platform is best for your organization? If you have a platform already, what will you do to make it work for you?

8. How will you measure progress?

9. How do you plan to tell your organization about successes?

# CHAPTER 6

# The Rule of Overcoming Bias

**TWITTER SUMMARY ≤ 140 CHARACTERS**

Many people have biases toward new ways of learning. Overcome them by eliminating fears and filling knowledge gaps about technology.

*After speaking at a conference focused on corporate elearning, a participant approached us with a question: "My boss won't change. She believes that people can't be taught if training isn't a face-to-face experience conducted in a brick-and-mortar building. How can I help her see that this isn't the case?"*

Many people are preconditioned to think this way. Their beliefs are sometimes rooted in a more traditional way of thinking, making their biases hard to overcome. They often just need exposure to new concepts.

Adhering to one's own point of view when processing new information is a fairly common practice. Even the following well-respected and highly influential individuals had narrow vision:

- "The earth is at the center of the universe." —Ptolemy, 150 CE

- "The 'telephone' has too many shortcomings to be seriously considered as a means of communication. The device is inherently of no value to us."—Western Union, 1881

- "The horse is here to stay, but the automobile is only a novelty."—President of the Michigan Savings Bank, 1903

- "Television won't be able to hold onto any market it captures after the first six months. People will soon get tired of staring at a plywood box every night."—Darryl F. Zanuck, President of 20th Century Fox, 1946

- "Man will never reach the moon regardless of all future scientific advances."—Lee de Forest, inventor of the radio tube, 1967

We could also add the following statement made by so many:

- "The virtual classroom will never replace traditional face-to-face training."

## Leader Biases

When it comes to prejudice against virtual classrooms, we have found that there are four types of biased leaders:

1. Turf Protectors
2. Creatures of Habit
3. Nail-Biters
4. The Unenlightened

These individuals have the influence to make or break your project. Hence, it's critical to know how to persuade them in favor of your cause. We recognize that in many instances, you will need to vigorously defend the decision to move your training online.

*David Smith, a master facilitator at InSync Training located in Leeds, England, confirms this sentiment. "When we deal with prospects who have never considered virtual-classroom training before, we are very much on an education mission," says Smith. "Many organizations find it difficult to consider live virtual-classroom training because of the mind-set of 'How can it possibly claim to replace or be as good as face-to-face training?' Often the best response is to provide them with the experience of being in a live virtual-classroom session, and the doubts start to evaporate immediately."*

## 1. Turf Protectors

Turf Protectors feel threatened. They believe a new idea is going to take away their position, their job, or the perception that they are the oracles of all learning within the organization. You may also refer to them as Luddites—a term that came about in the early 19th century to describe people opposed to technological change out of fear for their jobs.

To help overcome this issue, you should arm yourself with the facts. Show the Turf Protectors that many people actually prefer to learn virtually and, more importantly, that it is effective. Do some research within your company. Also, find relevant secondary research from your industry in trade magazines and online to support your initiative.

For instance, you could share the following statistic from The Corporate Learning Factbook® 2010[29]:

> "The use of online methods for learning delivery increased in 2009 to one-third of total training hours consumed by learners. This increase came primarily at the expense of instructor-led classroom training (ILT)."

### Learning Fragment

**SMARTBRIEF.COM[30]**
Sign up to your industry's SmartBrief and receive frequent email newsletters with relevant data and trends you can use to support your cause.

Be prepared to really prove your case. Turf Protectors will often put up several barriers to keep out anything that may threaten their jobs or image. Here are a few examples:

| Barrier A | Your Response |
| --- | --- |
| "Online training won't make a difference in our organization." | "Taking our training initiatives online allows us to reach more workers with less cost. This medium can also be used as a reinforcement to live training, helping ensure that training sticks. Employees are very comfortable with online training. In fact, much of the time, this is their preferred training method." |
| **Barrier B** | **Your Response** |
| "Nothing is as effective as training done by a trainer in one of our classrooms." | "There is no question that face-to-face training is effective, but most people are surprised at how similar to a physical classroom this new delivery method can be. Learners still have the benefit of a live trainer to whom they can ask questions and receive feedback. Plus, the virtual classroom has many of the same features of a physical one like whiteboards, PowerPoint slides, and the ability to hold breakout groups. These rooms also have other great tools like polling features and chat boxes that help move interaction to a higher level." |

| Barrier C | Your Response |
|---|---|
| "We don't have budget to roll out virtual classrooms." | "Although there is typically a minimal start-up fee (usually under $1,500) there are zero travel costs for learners or instructors, which will easily offset the expense. We can also provide electronic handouts that will cut material costs. Additionally, the learners will spend less time away from their desks, which will increase their productivity." |
| **Barrier D** | **Your Response** |
| "You are very busy. Where are you going to find the time to do this? | "Getting started is not as difficult as you'd think, and it will fit easily into our current training model. I would expect a bit of ramp-up time and some time to modify the instructional design, but nothing that would adversely affect my job. In fact, the benefits of teaching this way—positioning our department as forward-thinking and cost-conscious—should only benefit us in the long run." |

## 2. Creatures of Habit

The Creatures of Habit are blind to what exists around them. They like the safety and familiarity of consistency. They rarely explore new and different ideas. Their eyes just need to be opened. One way to pry them open is to show them what your competition is doing and how far behind the curve your organization is falling. Contact friends who work for other organizations and find out how their training methods are changing and what sort of results they've had. Share this information with your leader in a considerate and courageous manner.

Another way to help the Creature of Habit see clearly is to create an alternate training method and determine which course people like to attend. For example, take your existing training methods, perhaps a full day

**Learning Fragment**

**LINKEDIN.COM, THE ELEARNING GUILD GROUP[31]**
Reach out to this professional network of colleagues to ask for their advice and suggestions on how they have successfully made the transition to the virtual classroom. You could also start a group discussion asking that exact question

of traditional classroom training, and also create a new virtual-classroom experience. Give your learners the choice of attending either. Then show your boss exactly what people liked and how effective the virtual-classroom option can be. If your experience is anything like ours, you'll see that many people will opt for the new virtual-classroom experience.

You'll soon find that you are able to reach your audience in a way that they want to learn—whether it be through convenience or learning style. You may also be able to reach people who couldn't attend or didn't want to attend training in the past. For example, we gave a subset of our learners the choice to attend a specific face-to-face training session or receive the same training online. Out of 2,433 people, 48.9 percent attended the ILT, while 51.1 percent attended via the virtual classroom.

### 3. Nail-Biters

If your leaders are anxious about virtual classrooms, it may be because they do not understand the technology. In almost every case, knowledge is the best treatment for this type of person. So teach Nail-Biters how it works— give them a shot of courage.

Find a way to unassumingly educate your boss on all the pros and cons of the new technology. An understanding of both the good and bad, with a little more focus on the good (of course), will remove fear of the unknown and all of the anxiety that comes with it. An easy way to do this is to set up an online demonstration with your technology vendor of choice. They are always happy to do demos to show off their products, and they are very knowledgeable on the topic. A little bit of expert knowledge will go a long way to relieve any anxiety.

### Learning Fragments

**HOWSTUFFWORKS.COM**[32]

**YOUTUBE.COM**[33]

Just type "virtual classrooms" into the search field of both websites and carefully review the many articles and videos on the subject. Find the best fragments for your specific need and forward them to your boss with a short introduction.

## 4. The Unenlightened

If your leaders aren't quick on the uptake, good luck. You'll probably need to go over their heads and talk with their boss. Or take your ideas to other business leaders within your organization who will serve as your champions. In some cases, having a boss like this can be a good thing—you might be able to carve out a niche within your organization that you will end up owning in the future.

If you don't think your organization will survive the Learning Explosion without transitioning to the virtual classroom and you are managed by an unenlightened boss, we recommend you start looking for a new job. Or put together a solid argument based on research you have gathered from other learning fragments and present your vision to your boss's boss. Who knows, you may even get a promotion!

---

### Learning Fragments

**INDEED.COM**[34]

**CAREERBUILDER.COM**[35]

**MONSTER.COM**[36]

Perhaps it's time to start looking for a job with an organization that understands the importance of online learning.

---

### Learner Biases

It's important to note that, just like leader biases, many learners possess similar prejudices. They may not know the benefits of receiving training through new methods or they may actually fear the use of technology when it comes to learning. Over time, word of mouth from their colleagues will convince them to try new learning methods. But you can also speed up the process through some simple tactics.

- Schedule twice as many virtual sessions. When learners see that there are more options for training, it will have a positive impact on their already tight schedule.

- Simplify communication and procedures. If your learners are apprehensive about new technologies, try to keep everything very simple. Don't speak in technical jargon. Use basic terms they are familiar with and keep login instructions easy.

- Get executive endorsements. Now that your leaders understand the benefits of virtual training, ask them to provide compelling quotes about the importance of this new initiative, and communicate these frequently to your end users. Even better, have a directive come down from the executive ranks indicating that your virtual training is mandatory.

The fact remains that everyone has biases on which they operate and to which they default. But these biases can be changed with relevant knowledge.

If you are in the training or education industry, you understand that almost anyone can change with education. Is it always easy? No. But it is always worth the time and effort to watch someone become enlightened. It is why many of us do what we do. We like being the catalyst that facilitates that change in others. Sometimes this means being the conduit of knowledge to those to whom we report.

### Learning Fragment

For more research on and trends associated with the virtual classroom, refer to the list of sources we shared at the end of Chapter 1. Studies, reports, and statistics are an extremely effective tool in overcoming biases.

## Learning Explosion Action Plan

### THE RULE OF OVERCOMING BIAS

The answers to this action plan should probably be kept confidential. We wouldn't want you to lose your job because you referred to anyone as unenlightened.

1.  Think of your main leader(s).

2.  Circle the type of leader(s) you are dealing with.

    Turf Protectors

    Creatures of Habit

    Nail-Biters

    The Unenlightened

    Other: _____

3.  What learning fragments will you access to arm yourself with the data you need to prepare a solid argument for virtual classrooms?

    _____

    _____

4.  How do you plan on persuading your leader(s) to transition to the new virtual classroom?

    _____

    _____

5   What are some learner biases within your organization?

    _____

    _____

6.  How do you plan on overcoming them?

    _____

    _____

    _____

# CHAPTER 7

# The Rule of Virtual Accountability

## TWITTER SUMMARY ≤ 140 CHARACTERS

To facilitate effective behavior change and learning, you must hold learners virtually accountable—verbally, visually, and kinesthetically.

What are the first things that come to mind when you think of holding people accountable in a training or educational setting? You probably think of assignments, homework, or some other method that indicates a learner's understanding and proficiency in the material you have just taught them. Every good training event should have some form of accountability built into it.

## Nonverbal Accountability

In a live classroom or lecture-hall setting, your body is physically present. You are nonverbally accountable. In other words, your body language or nonverbal communication is visible to those around you, making you accountable for your physical actions. Some examples of acceptable nonverbal accountability are raising your hands when you know the answer to a question, nodding your head in agreement, smiling, or even laughing at an instructor's joke. Yes, laughter and other forms of paralanguage (the pitch, volume, and intonation of speech) are also classified as nonverbal communication.

Unacceptable nonverbal behavior in a live classroom would include falling asleep, laughing uncontrollably, making obscene gestures, talking on your cell phone, or listening to your iPod rather than the facilitator. Most people would not do any of these things for fear of being called out by the instructor or humiliated by peers. In a physical classroom setting, they are nonverbally accountable.

> *Now come with us to the dark office or cubicle of partici-pants attending a virtual classroom. You will most likely find them alone, staring at their computer screen. They are NOT nonverbally accountable. If they physically raise their hand, nod their head, smile, or laugh, it will be for their benefit only. There is no one to reprimand or chide them if they fall asleep or make a call on their cell phone. In fact, in many cases, no one would even know whether they slept during the entire session or not. In addition, they are not paying for a flight, hotel room, and daily per diem for this training experience, so they do not feel socially, ethically, and/or financially respon-sible to be attentive or alert.*

In this example, you can see how the very thing that makes online learning a strength can also be its weak-ness. So now that we have painted a fairly negative pic-ture, what can we do about it?

## Holding Learners Virtually Accountable

If you want your learners to be active participants in your virtual classroom and actually change behavior, then you must hold them accountable in three ways: verbally, visually, and kinesthetically.

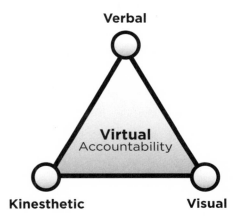

**VIRTUAL ACCOUNTABILITY MODEL**

A quick reminder. While we will share with you some proven methods to hold your learners virtually accountable in this chapter, there are so many other methods available through additional learning-fragment sources online. Some we will continue to share with you through the various Learning Explosion resource sites, but there are so many more still waiting to be discovered and shared.

## Verbal Accountability

In a virtual classroom, even though you do not have the benefit of holding your audience nonverbally account-able, you can still hold them verbally accountable.

*If we were to shout, "Marco," how would you reply? If you were born in the United States or in most countries belonging to the British Commonwealth, you would most likely respond with "Polo." That's because you have been conditioned to do so by playing the kids' game by that name.*

*In the game "Marco Polo," someone is typically selected to be "It." That person is either blindfolded or has to keep his or her eyes closed while trying to catch other players in the game. The child tries to catch others by shouting, "Marco," to which the other players must reply with "Polo." This allows "It" to verbally track down the other players in the game and tag them so they can pass on the "It" status.*

The game "Marco Polo" is a prime example of verbal accountability. Someone says one thing and you feel compelled to reply. Another example is saying, "Hello, how are you?" which almost always elicits "Fine, and you?" This same rule applies to the virtual classroom. If you condition your learners appropriately, they will feel accountable to respond to the various verbal cues and directions you give them.

## Conditioned [kuhn-dish-und] -noun

Characterized by a predictable or consistent pattern of behavior or thought as a result of having been subjected to certain circumstances or conditions.[37]

## Ten Methods to Create Verbal Accountability

*1* **The power of clear expectations.** People generally like to know what is expected of them in any given learning setting, informing them what behaviors are appropriate or not. So, in your virtual classroom, prepare your audience right up front with the expectation that you will hold them verbally accountable. Say something like, "I will be calling on you throughout the virtual classroom, sometimes by name, to answer some questions verbally. Please feel free to speak up if you have a comment or question." Then make sure you meet the expectations yourself.

2. **The "first" question.** The first time you ask a question and request a verbal answer, slowly count to 15 without saying a word. It will be very uncomfortable at first. You cannot see your audience, and you may wonder if they are even there. But by doing this one thing, you are conditioning your audience to know that you are serious about holding them verbally accountable. If you jump in and answer the question yourself, you have immediately conditioned your audience to not be verbally accountable. Repeat this practice as often as necessary. Usually, it works after the first question.

3. **Be creative with verbal interactivity.** Build in frequent opportunities for verbal interaction. We recommend some form of verbal interaction at least every two to three minutes. One of FranklinCovey's virtual-classroom instructors, Dave Green, has a motto we ascribe to: "Interaction beats distraction," and verbal interaction is one way of accomplishing this. Another of FranklinCovey's expert virtual-classroom instructors, Mike Wuergler, actually teaches a principle by singing a short song and then asks participants to repeat it with him.

4. **Use people's names.** In a physical classroom, you may not like to call on people to answer a question for fear of putting them on the spot and potentially embarrassing them. However, we have found this to be different in the virtual-classroom envi-

ronment. In all the years we have tested this form of verbal accountability, we haven't ever had anyone get offended or upset, and rarely will anyone turn down the request to contribute. We have learned that while the same introverted personalities would be highly embarrassed to be put on the spot in a traditional classroom setting, they are typically just fine when called on in a virtual classroom. Why the difference? Because no one is looking at them. They do not feel the anxiety that comes from speaking in public. To them, it may feel like they are alone, just talking to a computer screen. There is no nonverbal embarrassment or phobia. You may be hesitant to try this at first, but we highly recommend this as a staple in your virtual classrooms.

## Real-World Example

### CALLING ON PEOPLE BY NAME

"At first, I was hesitant about calling on specific people by name to answer questions or share opinions," said Kelly O'Hara Bita, Senior Training Consultant at InterContinental Hotels Group. "I didn't want to put anyone on the spot. I would just throw a question out there and hope that the uncomfortable silence would finally get someone in virtual space to speak up. It was often painful and I ended up just answering for them."

"Now that I am letting people know up front that I will be calling on individuals throughout, they are ready to share," she continues. "I always make sure that the first question is asked of someone with whom I already have rapport. They are usually enthusiastic and it sets a good example for future victims I call on."

**⑤ Request elaboration.** Ask specific individuals to verbally elaborate on comments they have posted in the chat box and other tools in your virtual classroom. This not only shows that you are reading their comments, but it effectively conditions your learners to be engaged kinesthetically as well as verbally.

**⑥ Ask open-ended questions.** This is Training 101. Just like face-to-face training, if you want good discussion, ask open-ended questions.

**⑦ Reinforce through role play.** Hold your learners verbally accountable by asking for volunteers to role-play with you. You can ask them pre-planned questions related to the content you have just taught or for an exercise they have completed on their own. It's a great way to reinforce concepts and principles and make them relevant. To keep those learners who are not directly involved in the role play accountable, ask them to be prepared to provide their verbal feedback after the exercise.

**⑧ Try breakout sessions.** Some virtual-classroom platforms like WebEx and Adobe Connect have the ability to group learners into breakout rooms. This allows learners to work on specific questions or assignments in small groups and then report back verbally to the whole group.

**⑨ Discourage the "mute" button.** If you are conducting the audio portion of your virtual classroom with the help of a teleconference service, tell your learners not to mute their phones. This conditions them to understand that you expect their verbal accountability. Obviously, if they are in a noisy area, they may need to mute. Many platforms give facilitators the ability to mute learners who are in noisy environments. For those platforms that do not give facilitators this control, you are taking a risk of background noise. In our opinion, it's a risk worth taking because you will get much more verbal interaction from participants.

We have overseen the training of tens of thousands of people, and only in a very small percentage of cases have we had a bad experience—like the guy who went to the restroom with his cordless phone in his pocket, or the lady who was yelling at her kids, or the couple who got into a very personal argument. In these instances, mute would have been very nice, but then again, we would not have these war stories to tell.

Most potential problems can be averted with some preemptive conditioning. For example, make sure you clearly explain to your audience the pros and cons of leaving the phone off mute. Say something like, "Remember, we can hear you if you go to the restroom." And have every person in the virtual classroom verbally acknowledge that he or she has heard and understands the risks.

**Verbal Responsibility.** If you wish to hold your learners verbally accountable, you, the instructor, must also be verbally responsible. Let's elaborate on this statement with a real-world example on the next page.

If you remember to condition your learners appropriately and utilize these 10 methods of verbal accountability, your virtual classroom will be an easier place in which to learn and to instruct.

## Real-World Example

### BE VERBALLY RESPONSIBLE

Renee Tomlinson is a fantastic virtual-classroom instructor. She has a knack for knowing how to involve learners and facilitate discussion. However, on one occasion, she had accidentally overlapped her virtual-classroom event with an important business trip. She looked at the schedule and thought she could squeeze her virtual classroom in at the airport parking via her wireless card.

The day came, and according to plan, Renee found herself set up with her computer and headset in her car. Toward the end of the session, a family in a large diesel truck pulled up right beside her, and the father started revving the already noisy engine while the children yelled and played around the truck. Needless to say, her event was compromised because she was not verbally responsible. Renee never made that mistake again.

In other words, try to ensure you are in a controlled and reliable environment so that you can focus on your learners and not have to worry about what's going on around you.

## Visual Accountability

In action movies, you have a hero who is capable of the most amazing feats. Someone needs to be rescued from certain death at great risk to the hero, or a bomb needs to be defused to prevent a global catastrophe. What makes these scenes more tense is the fact that the hero is not usually equipped for the emergency and must rely on directions from an actual expert on his mobile phone. The dialogue typically goes something like this:

*Hero: "I've opened the bomb casing."*

*Bomb Expert: "Okay, how many wires do you see?"*

*Hero: "Three."*

*Bomb Expert: "What colors are they?"*

*Hero: "Green, red, and blue."*

*Bomb Expert: "Where is the blue wire going?"*

*Hero: "To the timing fuse."*

*And so the scene continues until the bomb is miraculously defused with only a second or two to spare.*

This is an example of visual accountability. In this example, if the hero doesn't accurately report what he sees and experiences, there will be a major disaster. Obviously, the consequences for not keeping someone visually accountable in a virtual classroom are not life-or-death, but there are still consequences. The most apparent outcome is that there will not be any change in the learner's behavior, which is typically the objective of training.

## Five Methods to Create Visual Accountability

(1) **Visually orient learners.** Along with verbally establishing clear expectations right up front, you should also give a visual orientation of how your learners can use the tools in the virtual-classroom platform to interact and participate. For example, you could create a short virtual-classroom etiquette video that is played at the beginning of each class. You may also want to take time to describe and explain the features

and functions and how to navigate within the virtual classroom.

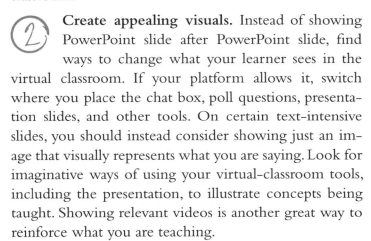

**Create appealing visuals.** Instead of showing PowerPoint slide after PowerPoint slide, find ways to change what your learner sees in the virtual classroom. If your platform allows it, switch where you place the chat box, poll questions, presentation slides, and other tools. On certain text-intensive slides, you should instead consider showing just an image that visually represents what you are saying. Look for imaginative ways of using your virtual-classroom tools, including the presentation, to illustrate concepts being taught. Showing relevant videos is another great way to reinforce what you are teaching.

**Learning Fragment**

**ENCYCLOMEDIA.COM**[38]
Choose from the thousands of free videos available on this site to incorporate into your virtual-classroom experience.

**Request visual accountability.** Ask your learners to account for what they are seeing in the virtual classroom. For example, if you are teaching bank employees how to identify suspicious customer behavior in their lobby, you could display several pictures showing various scenarios and ask them to identify potential concerns. In doing so, you keep learners actively engaged and accountable instead of passively present. It could mean providing an unfinished model or diagram and asking learners to identify what is missing.

You may also ask them to read a quote in the room or from participant materials they have in front of them.

 **Tell stories.** We call this the "picture this" principle. We realize that this could very easily go under verbal accountability, but bear with us, and you'll understand why we placed it here. It's amazing what can be conjured up by using your imagination. That's why we almost always enjoy the book more than the movie. The images we invent in our mind are much more lucid and relevant to our life experiences and preferences. Why not take advantage of this incredible talent that exists inside every person? Try asking your learners to "picture this" instead of showing them some clip art. To do this effectively, you need to carefully prepare the right words in the right sequence with the right dramatic flair, or else your learners may find the exercise "hokey" or "cheesy." While this may seem very much like storytelling in an ILT setting, remember that you do not have the benefit of nonverbal communication and, therefore, you rely much more on a combination of words and delivery. On the other hand, if you do not feel comfortable with this style of delivery, you could always share an image with them and then ask them to share what comes to mind. Either way, you are engaging them visually.

**Learning Fragment**

**AWESOMESTORIES.COM**[39]
Choose from thousands of stories with relevant pictures, slide shows, videos, audio clips, documents, and other primary sources linked, in context, where you need them.

⑤ **Show the way.** Provide a visual road map. Just as it is good practice in an ILT workshop to provide a road map of where you are going and where you have been, the same applies to your virtual classroom. Learners like to have their bearings about them in any type of training. If possible, try not to use bullet points as your road map. A clean, graphical model or image works best. However, bullets are better than not having anything at all.

When considering what visual elements to use to create accountability, try not to force visual stimuli on people. Be careful not to overdo it.

While images have the ability to hold your learners accountable, they can just as easily be a distraction. So keep your images relevant or leave them out. And remember that charts, graphs, and other diagrams are also viable options.

## Learning Fragments

### VISIONJAR.COM[40]

Johanna Rehnvall's focus is on visual communication. Her blog is a delightful collection of presentation design and other visual communication resources. She also has an extensive list of other related presentation sites.

### COMMONCRAFT.COM[41]

Enjoy these three-minute, paper-cutout videos that introduce complex subjects. See what relevant subjects they already have, or have them create your very own customized Common Craft video that you can use before, during, or after your virtual classroom.

## Kinesthetic Accountability

Use your imagination to picture the following situations:

1.  Try teaching someone how to use a yo-yo without using your hands.

2.  Try giving directions without pointing.

3.  Try getting someone's attention at a sporting event without waving your arms.

Frustrating, right? While we could all probably complete these activities without using body movement, it would take much longer and could be difficult. If we all learn so much better when we involve movement, then we should attempt to do the same in our virtual classrooms.

## Five Methods to Create Kinesthetic Accountability

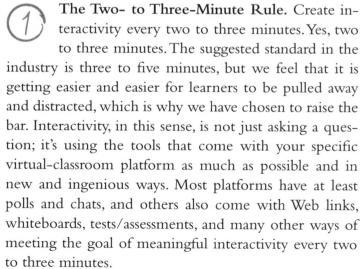

**The Two- to Three-Minute Rule.** Create interactivity every two to three minutes. Yes, two to three minutes. The suggested standard in the industry is three to five minutes, but we feel that it is getting easier and easier for learners to be pulled away and distracted, which is why we have chosen to raise the bar. Interactivity, in this sense, is not just asking a question; it's using the tools that come with your specific virtual-classroom platform as much as possible and in new and ingenious ways. Most platforms have at least polls and chats, and others also come with Web links, whiteboards, tests/assessments, and many other ways of meeting the goal of meaningful interactivity every two to three minutes.

**Hands-On Materials.** Providing downloadable or hard-copy materials is another effective means of mixing up how your learners are held kinesthetically accountable. This way, they have a valuable supplement and tool in front of them during the virtual-classroom experience. You can now build in opportunities throughout your virtual experience for them to complete a questionnaire, take notes, or just read a quote. These materials are a great tangible addition to the virtual experience, and something learners can take away from it.

**Use emoticons.** These are the icons available in your virtual classroom that allow your learners to express themselves electronically in fun ways. Emoticons include the ability for learners to raise their hand electronically, laugh at something the facilitator said, ask the facilitator to speed up or slow down, and other wonderful expressions. Each platform has some form of these cute little interactive tools. Look for ways to use them. For example, you could ask your learners to raise their hand when they have finished an offline activity, or you could have them select the "check mark" or "x" to indicate whether they agree or disagree with a statement you have just read.

**Provide short offline activities.** In some cases, the best way for someone to learn a new concept is to actually get up and do it. That means leaving the safety of the virtual classroom to venture into the real world and complete a task, then return and report what they discovered. This form of kinesthetic exercise requires four guidelines. You take a risk of losing people if you choose to do this exercise, but depending on what it is you want them to learn, it may be worth it. See the guidelines below.

## Offline-Activity Instructions

| 1. Set Clear Instructions | Verbally tell participants what you want them to do, reinforcing the instructions with a PowerPoint slide. Be sure participants also have a hard copy of the instructions in their downloadable or hard-copy materials. |
|---|---|
| 2. Convey Intended Outcomes | Before setting them free, be sure participants understand what the intended outcomes of the exercise are and what they will need to report on after the activity. |
| 3. Keep It Short | Don't give them more than five minutes offline. Make sure they have enough time to complete the exercise, but not so much time that they get sidetracked or pulled away for good. |
| 4. Report Out | Have each person report on what he or she learned. If you don't do this, the next time you try a similar exercise, they won't complete it. Rather, they will choose to engage in distractions, like answering email, rather than being in the virtual classroom. |

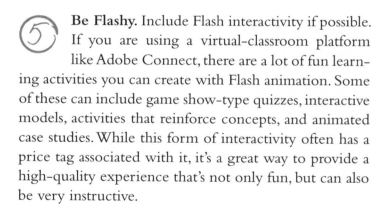 **Be Flashy.** Include Flash interactivity if possible. If you are using a virtual-classroom platform like Adobe Connect, there are a lot of fun learning activities you can create with Flash animation. Some of these can include game show–type quizzes, interactive models, activities that reinforce concepts, and animated case studies. While this form of interactivity often has a price tag associated with it, it's a great way to provide a high-quality experience that's not only fun, but can also be very instructive.

### Future Kinesthetic Tools

You may want to ask yourself how Kinect for Xbox 360 or the Nintendo Wii can factor into your learning. These and other technologies incorporate movement in incredibly innovative ways. If you are responsible for

## Learning Fragments

### ELEARNINGINTERACTIONS.COM[42]

This product by eLearning Brothers makes is easy for you to build Flash interactions you can use in your next virtual classroom. Choose from a library of interactions and themes to make your learning more engaging.

### VUVOX.COM[43]

Vuvox enables you to easily turn photos, videos, text, and audio clips into interactive stories. Create interactive collages that can be embedded into your virtual classroom or related website, blog, or social-networking site.

### DIPITY.COM[44]

Dipity is a free, digital timeline website. You can create, share, embed, and collaborate on interactive, visually engaging timelines that integrate video, audio, images, text, links, social media, location, and timestamps. Create your own timeline as it relates to the content in your virtual classroom.

teaching skills and techniques that include some form of movement, then you should probably be taking careful note of these types of technologies. Your virtual learners could benefit greatly by replicating what they just learned in the convenience of a digital environment. Thanks to these products, movement simulation and reinforcement can now be packaged up into small boxes, shipped anywhere in the world, and set up very easily. Some industries, like medical and government sectors, already use these forms of "active" learning technologies in training.

While these three accountability strategies may seem like a lot more work than just lecturing for two hours, you'll be rewarded with active participation and a quality training experience. Remember, your learners have more interesting distractions they can turn to if you can't offer them a better alternative.

## Learning Explosion Action Plan

### THE RULE OF VIRTUAL ACCOUNTABILITY CHECKLIST

1. Review this checklist before teaching your next scheduled virtual-classroom session.

2. After teaching, return and see how you did.

### VERBAL ACCOUNTABILITY

| | |
|---|---|
| ◯ | I have set up clear verbal expectations. |
| ◯ | I counted to 15 after asking the first question. |
| ◯ | I have built frequent verbal interactivity into the outline. |
| ◯ | I am calling people by name. |
| ◯ | I am asking my participants to verbally elaborate on comments they may have made in chats or other virtual-classroom tools. |
| ◯ | I am asking open-ended questions. |
| ◯ | I have created role-play opportunities. |
| ◯ | I am using "breakout" sessions (if my platform allows it). |
| ◯ | I am discouraging participants from "muting" their phones. |

### VISUAL ACCOUNTABILITY

| | |
|---|---|
| ◯ | I have lots of different kinds of visual stimuli. |
| ◯ | I have built in opportunities to request visual accountability. |
| ◯ | I use stories to engage learners. |
| ◯ | I have a road map. |
| ◯ | I have created a verbally responsible environment. |

## Learning Explosion Action Plan

### THE RULE OF VIRTUAL ACCOUNTABILITY CHECKLIST (CONT.)

#### KINESTHETIC ACCOUNTABILITY

- ○ I have interactivity at least every two to three minutes.
- ○ I have downloadable materials.
- ○ I make effective use of emoticons.
- ○ I have short offline exercises.
- ○ I have included Flash interactivity.

#### NOTES

# CHAPTER 8

# The Rule of Personal Practice

> ## TWITTER SUMMARY ≤ 140 CHARACTERS
>
> You may already know that you need to practice, but do you know how? Proficiency, observation, imitation, and personalization are keys.

As you have most likely noticed already, moving to the virtual classroom will require you to learn new skills based on a completely new set of tools. This will take time and devotion on your part. At times, it may seem difficult; other times, it might be monotonous. But in the end, it will be worth it.

We often ask facilitators in our conferences or training how long it took them to prepare before their first face-to-face training session. People's answers range from days to even weeks, depending on what they had to teach. They also share what motivated them to prepare so much. The two main reasons were a desire to do it right and fear of being unprepared. The same goes for teaching in a virtual classroom. Not only do you need to know the subject matter, you also need to learn a new way of teaching.

*From Matt: My 11-year-old son just joined the track team at his school. After his first day of practice, I asked how it went. "Hard," he replied. I reminded him of all of the 5Ks we had run together and how hard those were at times. Typically, toward the end of these races when our energy had diminished, I taught him to repeat a mantra to himself: "My name is Will Murdoch. I am a runner. I choose to do hard things. I do hard things so that they become easy." Had he not had the practice of the 5Ks, running wouldn't have become easier and enjoyable. Most certainly, he wouldn't have gone out for the track team.*

As you move your corporate classroom online, your initial experience will be much like Will's—hard. But with practice and time, it becomes easier. This is, in essence, the Rule of Personal Practice.

This rule has received quite a lot of coverage over the past few years from both Malcolm Gladwell and Geoff Colvin in their books *Outliers*[45] and *Talent Is Overrated*,[46] respectively.

Gladwell suggests that you can become an expert at something after 10,000 hours; Colvin indicates it takes 10 years. While we hold these theories to be true, we also believe that you do not need to practice for 10,000 hours or for 10 years before you can be considered an effective virtual-classroom instructor. However, we do believe that the simple principle of "practice makes perfect" is true.

We have witnessed what happens when facilitators practice—and when they don't. We're not saying you need to eat, breathe, and sleep in your virtual classroom. But we are saying that you need to be comfortable enough in this new environment that you won't get flustered when something unexpected happens, and that you'll be able to work the controls just like you drive a car.

To be successful as a virtual instructor, we propose four stages of personal practice: platform proficiency, facilitator observation, imitation, and personalization.

## 1. Platform Proficiency

*From Treion: When I moved to the United States from South Africa, I never thought language would be a barrier. After all, I grew up speaking English. However, it became readily apparent that the English I was accustomed to was not the same as that spoken by new friends.*

*For instance, while driving from the airport with a girl I just met, I made a statement that is very common in South Africa. Used to driving on the other side of the car and on the other side of the road, I was startled by a large semitrailer truck and instinctively asked the girl who was driving to "honk her hooter at the truck." She immediately flushed and stopped talking. It was later that day when I learned that in America, you "honk your horn" and not your hooter.*

*In South Africa, honking your horn is also a very common means of communication between drivers. Not so in America. This was unfortunately just one of many embarrassing experiences I had regarding language differences.*

In some ways, learning new software is like learning a new language. To do so effectively, you immerse yourself in it until you truly understand it. Our hope is that you will become proficient in your new-platform language before you have any embarrassing experiences.

Every virtual-classroom platform has a variety of tools to help with your facilitation. Whatever your platform of choice, become proficient with all of the tools your platform provides. Each platform, from Adobe Connect to Citrix® GoToTraining™, has its own cache of interactive tools that are often underutilized. Experiment with every button on the screen so you know what happens if you push it.

We also recommend you set up a second computer to reflect what your participant sees. That way you experience how the tools affect the participant's screen as well. Review the following learning fragments to learn about some of the leading virtual-classroom platforms and their tools.

## Leading Virtual-Classroom Platforms

| Virtual-Classroom Platform | Learning-Fragment Resource |
|---|---|
| Adobe® Connect™ | Adobe Connect Resource Center[47]—access to self-paced tutorials, best-practices articles, and tips and tricks. |
| Cisco® WebEx® | WebEx MyResources Page[48]—access to video demos, articles, and other support resources. |
| Citrix® GoToTraining™ | GoToTraining[49] page and Citrix Knowledge Center[50]—access to hotfixes, security bulletins, troubleshooting guides, communities, and blogs. |
| Microsoft® LiveMeeting® | Microsoft LiveMeeting Resource Center[51]—access downloads, white papers, and demos. |

We also recommend you use a technical copilot at first. If you have the benefit of knowing a platform expert, have that person attend your virtual classrooms until you feel confident. This will free you up to focus on the content flow and allow you to create an interactive experience. You will also be able to see how the technology works in a real-world situation. However, try not to be copilot-dependent for too long. We have found that you can become platform-proficient very quickly. You just need to immerse yourself in the technology.

### Understanding Technical Basics

Becoming very comfortable with the platform is important, but being proficient enough to solve common technical issues is imperative. This is usually where we lose some of you. Every time we mention the word "technical," some trainers automatically dismiss themselves as "not very good with computers and technical stuff," and they check out.

If this is you, please do not skip over this section quite yet. We have good news for you.

Many other trainers who have had the same opinion of themselves, have successfully made the transition, and are now quite expert when it comes to "technical stuff." As a matter of fact, one of the authors is a living example of this transformational phenomenon. (To find out who, go to the section about the authors at the end of the book).

Previously, in the Rule of Overcoming Bias, we stated that knowledge was the best treatment for a fear of technology. The same is true here. To help you get you on your way to technical proficiency, we have provided what we feel are the most common technical issues and a general solution to each. Please also refer to the "Leading Virtual-Classroom Platform" resources already referred to in this section to gain specific knowledge and answers to your platform's unique challenges and issues.

## Common Technical Watchouts

| Potential Issue | Solution |
|---|---|
| Learners cannot get into the virtual classroom. | 1. Verify that they have the correct login instructions.<br><br>2. Have them disable their pop-up blocker. Their browser could be blocking the page or preventing them from downloading required software.<br><br>3. Have them check the "technical requirements" associated with your platform. Send out these requirements before the event or make it available to your learners online. (Each platform can provide this information for you.) |
| The Internet connection is weak. | 1. Test your network connection beforehand. Do this by going to speedtest.net. You want to ensure that you and your learners are accessing a reliable network.<br><br>2. Try not to use a wireless connection to facilitate or participate in a webinar. Wireless can be unreliable, and in many cases, just plain bad. |
| A firewall is blocking the platform. | Work with your IT group beforehand to ensure your firewall will allow you and your learners to access your virtual-classroom platform. |
| How do I orient a learner to the platform? | Refer to the aforementioned "Leading Virtual-Classroom Platform" resources for specific tutorials and PDF downloads you can share with your learners. |
| Videos and/or PowerPoints are choppy. | 1. Ask your learners to shut down any applications, programs, and/or software that could be taking up valuable bandwidth on their computer systems.<br><br>2. Ensure that your learners have a better connection than dial-up.<br><br>3. Work with your IT beforehand on testing how much bandwidth your virtual-classroom events will require.<br><br>4. Compress the videos down to about 640 pixels by 480 pixels to reduce the amount of bandwidth needed. Use YouTube as a guide. If learners can play YouTube videos on their computer, then they should be able to play 640 by 480 videos. |
| Learners receive an Adobe® Flash® error. | This is easily addressed by directing them to the Adobe Flash website where they can download the latest version for free. It only takes a moment, and they should be able to join the webinar in a timely manner. The link to download the latest version is http://get.adobe.com/flashplayer. |

*Have a Backup Plan*

While technology has become more reliable over the past few years, the unexpected hiccup is still possible. No matter what your technical proficiency, sometimes things will still go wrong—things you have no control over that cannot be fixed: your network could go down, the power could go out, or your computer could blow up. In these rare scenarios, we advise having a backup plan in place. Be sure to accurately communicate the plan with all of the participants. Some basic suggestions could include:

- Move the event to another day. This is probably the easiest option, but it is often not the most convenient one.

- Record the event as soon as you can and send the recorded link to your learners.

- As a last resort, have a PDF version of the participant materials emailed to learners and have everyone call in to a teleconference line. This is a viable option if you have a deadline in which to teach your content. Obviously, the learner experience will not be as interactive and dynamic without the tools and visuals of a virtual classroom, but it will do.

**Learning Fragment**

**ONLINE BOOK OF INSTRUCTIONS**
"Twenty Things I Learned About Browsers and the Web" is a great example of how you can share not-so-exciting technical information—like a backup plan or technical FAQs—in an very interactive and visually appealing way.[52]

## 2. Facilitator Observation

Recently, we were talking with one of our clients who trains a global employee base at a multibillion-dollar company. We asked her about her experience teaching in a virtual classroom and how hard it was to get started.

"The problem was not mastering the platform. It took time, but I was able to master it," she said. "What surprised me was the challenge I had when it came to actually facilitating. I really had to monitor the awareness and the engagement of the group, and encourage their interaction despite the fact we weren't face-to-face."

She found it was helpful to watch someone else facilitate it first through a recording. She watched it several times. She also attended a virtual classroom called *Presenting Great Webinars* that covered virtual-classroom tips, tricks, and best practices.

Some proven methods of virtual-classroom observation are:

- Watching a recording of a subject-matter expert (SME) teaching the same content.

- Attending a live virtual classroom of that content.

- Sitting in the same room as the SME as he or she facilitates the virtual classroom.

> ### Real-World Example
>
> **KHAN ACADEMY**[53]
>
> Khan Academy's mission is to provide a world-class education to anyone, anywhere. Their method? Observation. Known as Bill Gates' favorite teacher, Sal Khan has successfully managed to create an environment where math students of all ages can go online and observe someone breaking down math problems. With a very intuitive interface, one man has been able to do what many have been trying to do for hundreds of years: simplify math. And his watch-and-learn approach is how he is accomplishing this great feat.

## 3. Imitation

Effective observation leads to the essential stage of replication, or imitation, of the behavior observed. Simply put, you must attempt to imitate what you liked by practicing with real people, not just by yourself.

Make sure you inform your practice audience that you not only want their critique and constructive criticism, but that you expect it. Take careful note of the things that go well and those that don't. Then practice again and again.

To aid with this step, we provide our virtual-classroom instructors with a tool: a very detailed facilitator guide or outline. The guide includes specific instructions on what to say, when to show a PowerPoint slide, and how to facilitate an exercise. If they choose to imitate how we suggest they teach the experience, they become confident enough to eventually personalize it.

## Real-World Example

### FACILITATOR-GUIDE INSTRUCTIONS

Here is a sample from *The 7 Habits Jump Start Series* facilitator guide. As you write your facilitator instructions, be sure you are very descriptive so that the instructor can imitate it as closely as possible.

1. After the video, show Slide 20, "The Circle of Influence Model."

2. State:

   Proactive people focus on things they can influence. Consider two circles. The inner circle represents things you can influence and change: your attitude, your actions, your choices.

   The outer circle represents the thousands of things that concern you, but which you can't really do anything about. Reactive people spend a lot of time and energy worrying about things in which circle? Yes, the outer circle. As a result, they lose power and feel like victims of circumstance. If you focus on the inner circle—the things you can influence—you'll strengthen your "proactive muscle" and ultimately have greater power and control over your life.

3. Ask:

   Which circle do you think reactive people spend more time in? Why?

4. Chat. Ask participants to answer verbally or in the chat pod: "What should the main character in the video we just watched do about the budget issue?"

5. Debrief responses.

6. State:

   If we consistently exercise our "proactive muscle," it will get stronger and our Circle of Influence will grow. Conversely, if we focus on reactivity, our Circle of Influence will decrease and our Circle of Concern will get larger.

## 4. Personalization

Once you have mastered the platform, observed a SME in action, and taken time to practice what you have learned, you can personalize the virtual-classroom experience with your own style and customized content. Make it your own. Make it something that you enjoy and that will promote your personality as well.

You'll be surprised at how easy it is to personalize your content once you have completed the other stages.

---

**Real-World Example**

**VIRTUAL CLASSROOMS TO THE RESCUE**

One of our clients had a critical need. They had to train 8,000 employees on a new financial system they were implementing, and do it in a very short time with an even smaller budget. So we introduced them to virtual classrooms. They liked our platform and instructional-design approach, but wanted to do it their own way.

Using our general approach as a base, we helped them personalize two custom sessions that specifically addressed their training needs and effectively trained their employees in the time provided and under budget.

The more each of their four instructors taught the classes, the more they personalized the experience, until they each made it his or her own.

---

Personalization doesn't always mean you need to overhaul your virtual classroom. You can also customize your content with simple things such as your own examples, anecdotes, and culturally specific stories and images.

Remember that repetition is the father of all learning. Practice-teaching and understanding your platform will help alleviate any anxiety you may have prior to teaching. There is no substitute for good preparation, and your attendees will be able to recognize this.

By the way, if you do eventually reach that 10,000-hour level, you will not only be an expert, but a verifiable Jedi of virtual classrooms. Contact us when you reach that milestone so we can talk to you about all you have learned.

## Learning Explosion Action Plan

### THE RULE OF PERSONAL PRACTICE

Take a moment to answer the following questions:

1. If you have a platform already, what is it?

2. How would you rate yourself on that platform?
   a. Expert
   b. Tweener
   c. Beginner

3. Who do you know that is an expert on your platform? If no one, to which learning fragment will you turn to find one?

4. When can you observe that expert teaching a virtual classroom?

5. How do you plan to imitate the best practices you observed?

6. How can you personalize your virtual classroom to meet the needs of your organization?

# CHAPTER 9

# The Rule of Thumbs Up

## TWITTER SUMMARY ≤ 140 CHARACTERS

People like leaving their mark and giving feedback if you make it easy for them to do. Use this feedback to improve your virtual classroom.

Ever since man has roamed the earth, he's wanted to leave his mark. In the case of the caveman, it was on a wall; for the Renaissance man, it was on paper; and for us, it is on the Internet. The Internet is a cave wall with unlimited space and coverage. Many of us are comfortable writing all over that wall and sharing our insights with total strangers.

Leaving our mark has become much easier, especially when it comes to what we like and dislike. Rating what we buy, consume, experience, and review is so ingrained into our virtual world that we don't hesitate about letting the world know what we think. Some of us will even take more time to write what we loved or hated about an experience than we took having the experience itself!

Some good examples of this feedback phenomenon are Foursquare and Gowalla, where you voluntarily offer up your unabashed feedback on any sort of product or service.

### Learning Fragments

**FOURSQUARE.COM**[54]
**GOWALLA.COM**[55]
Foursquare and Gowalla are mobile applications that primarily help you discover great places and share them with your friends.

Our point is that people, in general, like to leave their mark by giving feedback—especially online—and only if it's a seamless experience. So why not take advantage of this human tendency and apply it to your virtual classrooms? This is what the Rule of Thumbs Up is all about—giving people ample opportunity to share what they like and dislike so you can continuously improve your virtual-classroom experience.

To create an effective feedback process people will use and that you will benefit from, we recommend a five-step process.

- Make it easy to use.
- Keep it short.
- Listen and learn.
- Apply changes.
- Repeat often.

## 1. Make It Easy to Use

Your feedback tool should be easy for the learner to access and navigate. This is one area where we can learn a lot from ILT. Being in the training industry, you have probably become accustomed to providing and receiving feedback. The proverbial "feedback form" is usually on the chair or table waiting for learners at every conference and workshop you attend. You can easily get to it, understand it, and usually fill it out in minutes.

The same best practice should be applied to your virtual-classroom feedback tool. In other words, it should be found quickly and intuitively. Once a learner has the feedback tool or form, it should be easy to complete and submit.

Do not send them on a wild-goose chase across the Web. And please, do not email them a PDF document and ask them to fill it out, scan the completed form, and then email it back to you. We can guarantee that doing this will result in a very low percentage of people giving you feedback. Plus, it takes too long and is unnecessarily burdensome. Rather, there are several free and paid online-survey and collaboration tools you could use.

**Learning Fragments**

**SURVEYMONKEY.COM**[56]
SurveyMonkey makes it really easy for you to create a feedback survey, send it to whomever you wish, and then retrieve the tabulated data. Best of all, its free!

**ZOOMERANG.COM**[57]
Zoomerang also has a free, easy-to-use interface for creating and sending surveys.

## 2. Keep It Short

As we stated at the beginning of this book, keeping things short is one of the most important learning principles in today's media-rich world. Simplicity is what makes the most successful rating systems work. Just a couple of clicks and you're done. Have you ever been asked to participate in an online evaluation that had multiple pages and dozens of questions, only to quit halfway through?

To gather adequate feedback for your new virtual classroom, you may need to have more than two clicks, but use common sense and keep it short. We recommend asking between two and five questions that can easily be answered by your learners. Also, provide an option for people to add comments if they want to. Think carefully about the questions you want to ask and vet them through some trusted colleagues to give you their opinions.

---

**Real-World Example**

**THE ULTIMATE QUESTION**
At FranklinCovey, we ask two questions, based on Fred Reichheld's book *The Ultimate Question*.[58]

> Question 1: "How likely is it that you would recommend this experience to a friend or colleague?"

> Question 2: "What is the primary reason for the score you just gave us?"

---

Receiving answers to these simple questions lets you know whether or not your virtual classrooms are meeting your quality objectives. If the scores are low, you can take appropriate actions and measures to modify your experience.

### 3. Listen and Learn

Getting your learners to leave feedback is just half the process. You must now analyze the scores and comments to determine what changes need to be made—if any at all.

Look for recurring suggestions and patterns in what you're reading. Do people usually give you lower scores on one specific question? Is there a common theme with the comments people leave? If so, these are obviously the trouble areas you should focus on changing first. Also, beware of random and unusual suggestions and feedback. You've probably seen them before—the comments that are completely obscure, irrelevant, or that throw your entire course on its head.

When you receive these obscure comments, you can graciously ignore them. Set them aside as anomalies, or in some cases, even consider them, because occasionally, you will get a response that sparks a new idea or an innovative approach. Some of our best ideas have come from people in our virtual-classroom practice sessions who, in the spirit of constructive feedback, have shared new and better ways of doing things, which we have adopted.

## Real-World Example

### WHY DIDN'T WE THINK OF THAT?

As part of each new LiveClicks webinar launch, we make sure we comprehensively test the experience with our end users. On one occasion, we were nearing the launch date of a series of three webinars and were in the process of testing the final one, when a participant gave us some feedback that dramatically changed everything. That person simply asked why we needed three webinars when two would do. Initially, we thought this was an obscure comment and were ready to disregard it. We had already put a lot of time and effort into creating three, and no one else had made this suggestion before. But when we stopped and thought about it, we realized the participant was absolutely right, and we changed direction completely and ended up with two quality webinars. Imagine if that person hadn't had the courage to speak up or we hadn't had the smarts to listen? We may have had three fairly good webinars, but we are always in pursuit of greatness.

Listen and learn. You never know what you'll discover.

## 4. Apply Changes

Once you have sorted the feedback into what needs to be applied and what can be ignored, go ahead and make the changes to your virtual classroom. With all the changes made, you have an opportunity to create loyal fans. Contact those learners who gave you feedback to say thank you, and allow them to see how their suggestions were applied. The virtual classroom is now *their* virtual classroom because they had a say in how it was constructed.

## 5. Repeat Often

Schedule a set time to regularly go over your feedback process and continue to improve your virtual experience. Changing materials in a virtual classroom is generally easier to do than in ILTs. You don't have to deal with a printed product and inventory, so you can receive and apply feedback far more frequently.

### Real-World Example

**KEEPING WORKSHOPS FRESH**

At InterContinental Hotels Group (IHG), they understand the importance of feedback. Kelly O'Hara Bita, Senior Training Consultant, said, "We have a quarterly audit process in place for all of our workshops. Every 90 days, we analyze feedback from post-workshop surveymonkey.com surveys, obtain new information on the subject matter, and update our workshops to keep them fresh."

The Rule of Thumbs Up can be a very enjoyable and satisfying experience if done correctly. Your participant feedback is crucial to this process. So remember to tap into the experiences of your participants and utilize this information to continually improve your virtual classrooms so that you can keep getting the "thumbs up."

## Learning Explosion Action Plan

### THE RULE OF THUMBS UP

Ask yourself these questions to see if you have a great feedback process in place:

1. Is your feedback tool easy to find?

   _____

   _____

   _____

   _____

2. Can your feedback form be completed in under a minute if learners do not leave comments?

   _____

   _____

   _____

   _____

3. How often will you take time to listen and learn from the feedback you receive? Do you have time scheduled?

   _____

   _____

   _____

   _____

4. What system will you follow to apply the feedback you received?

   _____

   _____

   _____

   _____

   _____

# CHAPTER 10

# The Rule of Global Positioning

**TWITTER SUMMARY ≤ 140 CHARACTERS**

Reaching a global audience of learners is easy—and getting easier. But there are many barriers to be aware of before you apply for a visa.

## The Virtual Classroom Is Going Global

Imagine what it was like in the 1800s to see the spread of electric lighting around the world. We're seeing something equally as dramatic right now with the spread of the Internet.

While we recognize that not everyone works for a global company, we also believe that most of us will probably have the opportunity to collaborate in some way or another with global partners in the future.

So how global is the Internet really? To answer this question, we turned to a very enlightening learning fragment, Google Labs' Public Data Explorer. This fragment pulls data from the World Bank's collection of development indicators and presents the results in a fun, interactive graph.

**Learning Fragment**

**GOOGLE PUBLIC DATA EXPLORER**[59]
Take a couple of minutes to learn something new, right now, by going on this site to explore all of the fascinating data available, even down to the micro level.

The first thing we discovered was that the Internet hasn't been around as long as we all think, even though many of our children have never known

the world without it. Remember Y2K, when everyone thought our computers were going to crash at
the stroke of midnight? Well, only 6.8 percent of the
world's population had the Internet at that time. Compare that to 2008 where nearly a quarter of the world's
population was wired.

Using this learning fragment, we are also able to see
the Internet usage for every country. These statistics are
especially relevant if you're looking to launch virtual
classrooms to global markets. Let's look at some interesting national statistics and compare Internet usage among
several countries.

| Country | Wired Population (%) | Wired Population (#) |
|---------|---------------------|----------------------|
| Iceland | 90% | 300,000 |
| France | 67.9% | 42 million |
| India | 4.5% | 52 million |
| Brazil | 37.5% | 72 million |
| Japan | 75.2% | 96 million |
| United States | 75.9% | 231 million |
| China | 22.5% | 298 million |
| World | 23.5% | 1.59 billion |

*Source: 2008, http://www.google.com/publicdata/home.*

As you can see, Iceland leads the globe with 90 percent of its population wired with Internet connections.
However, that's fewer than 300,000 people. Compare
that with China, with nearly 300 million users, but only
22.5 percent of its population is connected.

For the first time ever, when we say "global," we really mean global. We recall the first day we conducted a virtual classroom with a group of people from South Korea. The following week we held one with people from Germany, then Australia, then Brazil. One day we conducted a virtual classroom that included people from three continents simultaneously.

This type of diverse virtual-classroom experience is becoming commonplace. Not a day goes by when someone sitting in another part of the world attends virtual learning. And because we live in a global marketplace, the odds of you conducting a virtual classroom with global attendees is very likely.

## Potential Global Barriers

As you explore going global, you need to be aware of the pitfalls that may limit your chances for success. More importantly, you need to be adaptable.

We've traveled around the world visiting countries in Asia, Latin America, Europe, and the Pacific Islands setting up organizations with virtual classrooms. In each location, we encountered something unique to that country that required rethinking our strategy. We never knew what it was going to be—it was always a surprise! For example, we were in a hotel in New Delhi trying to demonstrate a new virtual-classroom platform, but the power went out at least once every couple of hours. The funny thing is that our participants were used to it— they weren't fazed at all as they sat there patiently in the dark for a few minutes. We were a bit more concerned, however, wondering if our training session would need to be cancelled. Eventually, we got used to it and just rolled with the blackouts as they came.

In Costa Rica and other Latin American locations, the electricity generally worked fine, but the Internet bandwidth was often much slower than in other countries. You'll need to consider using lower-bandwidth products and services to reduce the drag on their systems.

### Learning Fragment

**SPEEDTEST.NET**[60]
With this learning fragment, you can have your international partners check the speed of their Internet connection at their respective locations. This will give you a very good idea of what you can and cannot share or stream in a virtual classroom.

In the Philippines and many other countries, including some in Europe, the government runs the telephone system, so getting a conference-call number for any type of audio training is really tough and sometimes cost-prohibitive! You'll need to consider Voice over IP (VoIP) in these instances if you are doing any sort of synchronous learning.

### Learning Fragment

**SKYPE.COM**[61]
If you are trying to launch virtual classrooms in one of these countries where getting a conference line is hard, try using Skype. In addition to conference calls within the same country, Skype gives you the ability to talk to anyone in the world from your computer or mobile phone, send SMS texts, conduct conference calls, use instant messaging, send and receive files, and even share your screen.

Of course, the largest barriers to successful implementation of your virtual classroom may be language and cultural differences. Often you will be blinded by your own culture. We can't stress enough the importance of having knowledgeable aides to help you navigate through these sometimes deep and complex waters. If you are going to be successful on a global level, you may need to relinquish some control to your international partners.

When we start a project, we always remind ourselves to "think global." This doesn't mean you simply slap on a picture of someone in a foreign country. It means you think about the culture and the language of the people you are trying to reach with your learning.

One of the great benefits to virtual classrooms is the speed at which you can localize your content. If you plan it correctly, you may be able to avoid hard-copy printed materials and only create electronic materials. Not only does this speed up production, but also think of the money saved. Imagine the potential cost savings you'll be able to share with your executive sponsors!

Localizing content can be tricky. To do it really well, we like to use people who actually live in the countries that are doing the delivery. We allow people in our global offices to take our raw files and localize them for their specific cultures. We have a great relationship with them and know that they will uphold our quality requirements. They understand their culture and can avoid images and language that may not portray reality or, even worse, would offend the learners. They are also able to do a better job translating materials than someone who is not a native speaker. Remember, a good-quality, localized product will help advance your project faster and more efficiently.

So when you decide to go global, try to be prepared, and remember that you will be met with a wide variety of situations for which you cannot plan—many of which you will never know exist until you experience them for yourself. Some of you may find these types of global situations exciting and adventuresome; for others, it will drive you crazy. You'll need to determine your capacity for embarking on this journey before you start. For us, it's been a lot of fun. The best advice we can give you is that when you begin your planning, plan to be flexible.

If you anticipate taking your virtual classroom global, use the following Learning Explosion Action Plan as a place to start.

## Learning Explosion Action Plan

### THE RULE OF GLOBAL POSITIONING

To apply the rule of global positioning, you can start by answering these key questions:

1. In what countries and languages would you want to localize your virtual classroom?

2. What is the speed of their Internet connection?

3. What raw files (PowerPoint, InDesign, Word, etc.) need to be localized?

4. Are there any special considerations you should be aware of when it comes to in-country utilities (power, telephone, Internet)?

5. Who can be your aide in understanding this? How will you schedule around these potential issues?

6. Do you have local presenters to teach your content in a virtual classroom, or will you be doing this from your current location? How will you account for time-zone differences?

7. What cultural topics and customs should you avoid? Which should you highlight? Who will help you know all of this?

.

# CHAPTER 11

# The
# Rule of
# Sustained
# Orbit

**TWITTER SUMMARY ≤ 140 CHARACTERS**

Getting your new virtual classroom off the ground is one thing. Achieving a sustained orbit is quite another.

We've talked about the Learning Explosion and how learning fragments are created. You now need to create a different type of explosion, one that will compress the explosion into a force to propel you forward. You need to be able to launch your virtual classrooms into orbit and keep them there.

There are a lot of things that will destroy your chances of getting your virtual classroom off the ground, but the biggest one is the law of gravity. It exists as much in the virtual world as it does in the physical world. This gravitational pull can be caused by other people's biases—like those telling us it can't or shouldn't be done, by budgetary restrictions, by a poorly planned and executed project, by a lack of focus, or simply by your own inertia. To succeed, you need to escape this gravitational pull. It will force you back into old ways of thinking. It will cause your projects to fail.

## What Is Orbit?

You have to define what your orbital level is—the point where gravitational drag ceases to weigh on your virtual-classroom initiative—and then recognize it when you get there. Is orbit defined by training a certain number of people each week? each month? each year? Is it generating a specific amount of revenue for your company each quarter? Is it eliminating a certain amount of travel expense? In some cases, you won't recognize that you're actually in orbit until you reach it.

With FranklinCovey LiveClicks webinar workshops, we've reached an orbital level that hopefully will keep up for quite some time. We know this because:

1. People are now asking for more virtual class-rooms.

2. It's generating enough revenue to sustain itself.

3. It's receiving executive approval and recogni-tion.

## Launching

To launch your virtual classroom, you need to have enough thrust to lift your project past the gravitational pull of the naysayers, your own insecurities, and the crazi-ness of your day job. You only have yourself and your team to provide the energy to get this done.

We've seen many virtual classrooms launched success-fully, but we've seen just as many fail. Some barely clear the launch pad before they crash back to earth. Some nearly reach orbit before burning up on reentry. What we've seen is that successful virtual-classroom launches come in two types: pure-force launches and critical-initiative launches.

### Pure-Force Launches

There are those projects that are thrust into orbit with im-mense force by a team of people who see the vision and do whatever they can to get it done. Think of President John F. Kennedy in 1961 proclaiming that we were go-ing to send a man to the moon by the end of that decade. With that vision and the sheer will of the NASA team, they were able to accomplish this incredible feat. As we reflect on our own virtual-classroom launches, we realize that we, too, achieved our goals through this same pure force and determination. There were many days where we just wanted to quit the projects because they were hard and we had so many other competing priorities. But we had a vision and we stuck to it.

A pure-force launch takes a tremendous amount of focus and dedication. It becomes very easy for launch dates to slip and for attention to be pulled to other projects. To help ensure that you succeed, you may want to have other people hold you accountable and act as your support team to keep you motivated. But at the end of the day, you must ultimately hold yourself accountable.

## Real-World Example

### PURE-FORCE LAUNCH IN INDIA

There is an enormous challenge in trying to train over a billion people with traditional ILT. Rajan Kaicker, executive chairman and managing director, and Lavleen Raheja, chairman and CEO of FranklinCovey India and South Asia, have a vision to help their countrymen become better at all aspects of their lives through highly effective training. They have an opportunity to provide much needed leadership and productivity skills throughout India. So they have turned to virtual classrooms to help expand their reach.

Rajan and Lavleen are involved in a pure-force launch. They were proactive by building their virtual-classroom learning circuitry (systems, processes, and capabilities) so they would be prepared when opportunities arose. Rajan and Lavleen also tasked their team to learn the technical and facilitation skills required to teach in this virtual world. To guarantee success, they set a launch date and drove everything toward it. Weekly team meetings were held to ensure they had all of the information necessary for a successful launch. In the end, they were well poised to accomplish their vision through virtual classrooms.

## Critical-Initiative Launches

The second method to get into orbit is due to a critical initiative. If you have to train 2,500 people around the world by next March, how will you do it? Mandates and urgency, like this, force you to think differently.

We've noticed that after our first successful launch, additional launches were much easier and faster. For instance, we had a client that needed a virtual-classroom solution immediately so they could train tens of thousands of people. This mandate forced us to get their virtual classroom on the launch pad and into orbit. We were able to meet this urgency because we already had a few successful launches behind us. We knew what could go wrong and we were able to course-correct quickly if anything did.

### Real-World Example

#### CRITICAL-INITIATIVE LAUNCH IN GERMANY

Alexandra Altman, CEO of FranklinCovey Leadership Institut GmbH, had an opportunity to bid on a large-scale project for a large company. The client was looking for a blended solution comprised of traditional ILT followed by two virtual classrooms. Her team was expertly prepared for the ILT portion of the project; however, they had not yet adopted virtual classrooms, but they were certain they could figure it out. They submitted their proposal and won the project. Now the client's urgency to deliver the training was high. They were about to experience a critical-initiative launch. They worked very hard to establish and learn the technology, as well as the facilitation skills needed to deliver the programs. They had to quickly build their learning circuitry and ensure the project was successful.

Because the deadline was imminent and unmovable by the client, it was easy for Alexandra and her team to keep focused on their virtual-classroom launch. Although their implementation timeline was very short, they were able to effectively launch their virtual classrooms and the client was very pleased with the results.

Be cautious, however, that you don't overpromise something to your customers. If you tell someone that you will have specific features or functionality and then can't deliver on it, you'll lose credibility. This is an easy trap to fall into if you are new to virtual classrooms. To avoid this, be sure to involve experts in your project and have them speak directly with your stakeholders or clients.

## Launch Training

Set a goal now to have flawless execution of your virtual classrooms. To do so, you'll need to train team members within your learning circuitry how to accomplish new tasks. There are two main categories of launch training you should be aware of: outreach and technical support.

### Outreach Training

Outreach training is directed to anyone who will be selling your solutions to stakeholders inside your organization or to buyers outside your organization. Volumes of books have been written on proper marketing communication, so we won't get into that here, but you need to have a plan to communicate to these people. We suggest a launch plan that includes, at a minimum, the following elements:

## Launch Worksheet

### *Pre-Launch Activities*

- Establish a list of team members and their responsibilities.
- Establish financials and create a pricing guide.
- Create flyers or brochures for your new service.
- Create internal and external frequently asked questions (FAQs).
- Create a product reference guide outlining the main features and benefits.
- Create technical-support materials for end users.
- Create a sales letter and email copy to be sent to prospective clients.
- Create scripts for your sales representatives.
- Develop and conduct sales training on how to position this service to clients.
- Conduct training for your operational teams and then test your ordering and fulfillment processes.

### *Launch Activities*

- Send out a press release or an internal memo.
- Conduct regular demonstrations of your virtual classroom for both internal stakeholders and potential buyers of your service.
- Collect early customer stories.

In addition to these tasks, we recommend you hold weekly pre-launch team meetings to ensure all members in your learning circuitry are being held accountable. You should also hold daily meetings after you've launched your virtual classrooms to fix any problems that have occurred and make quick repairs to your processes.

**Learning Fragment**

**CROSSING THE CHASM**[62]
In this book, you will learn the basics of communicating the value of your services to your stakeholders and your clients.

### *Technical-Support Training*

Technical-support training should be conducted for every team member, not just your technical-support team, because in the beginning, everyone will get calls from learners or instructors on how to troubleshoot certain issues. Make sure everyone is prepared by supplying them with hands-on training and a robust FAQ document. Most major virtual-classroom platforms have good technical-support sites with lots of relevant information. Provide your team members with the appropriate links and encourage them to also look at online forums if they have a problem they can't seem to resolve.

Remember that when you reach orbit, it's imperative to take time to celebrate. It's a wonderful feeling to be "weightless" outside the gravitational pull. But be careful. Even when you're in orbit, you can still be pulled back down. You need to make continual improvements and advancements in your virtual classroom to keep it flying: reenergizing it periodically with new and better courseware, branching out to new markets within or outside your organization, and taking time to improve your knowledge and awareness of the virtual-classroom industry so that you can keep your initiative in perpetual orbit.

## Learning Explosion Action Plan

### THE RULE OF SUSTAINED ORBIT

Ask yourself these 10 questions in order to successfully reach and sustain orbit.

1. What is propelling this launch—your vision and energy, or a specific initiative?

2. What is your deadline to launch your virtual classroom?

3. What are the success measures you must achieve in order to reach orbit?

4. Have you allocated ample time to this initiative?

5. How often will you and your team meet to discuss progress?

## The Learning Explosion Action Plan

### THE RULE OF SUSTAINED ORBIT (CONT.)

6. Have you created a scoreboard with critical measures? Do you update it regularly?

_____

_____

_____

7. What other projects will take time away from this project? How will you handle these competing demands on your time?

_____

_____

_____

8. What potential threats exist? What are your contingency plans to work around them?

_____

_____

_____

9. How will you communicate the initiative to your stakeholders (i.e., executives, clients, learners)?

_____

_____

_____

10. How will you handle technical-support issues when they arise?

_____

_____

_____

_____

# CHAPTER 12

# Caution!

## TWITTER SUMMARY ≤ 140 CHARACTERS

Learning will continue to change as new learning fragments are created. Be prepared to adapt, change, and grow.

Consider yourself warned. The rules shared in this book are forever changing. New technologies will be born, new needs will arise, new learning modalities will be invented, and new rules will be introduced.

**Beware!** The learning fragments that have been created by the Learning Explosion will continue to spawn more and more fragments—unfathomable quantities of fragments. You need to be able to adapt rapidly to new and relevant information as it becomes available. Remember to return to your learning fragments often to learn, modify, and improve as you move forward with online learning.

**Beware!** The tools you use today to deliver your virtual learning will be replaced with better tools tomorrow—tools that are more customized and more precise in their learning focus. You need to be prepared to adapt, evolve, and convert your learning to other tools as appropriate.

**Beware!** The success of your virtual-classroom programs depends on your instructors. These are the people who have the frontline interaction with the learners. If they fail to change their approach to content, length, instructional design, and delivery, the chance of failure increases substantially.

**Beware!** Some organizations may never rewire their circuitry to prepare for the virtual classroom. If you find yourself in this situation, you should seriously evaluate your options. Your transformative ideas may never take shape. You need to ask yourself if this is something you are willing to sacrifice. If not, you should reach out to other organizations that will benefit from your talents and ideas.

**Beware!** As long as there are humans, there will always be biases. Some people will never, ever change their attitudes around training modalities. To them, a physical classroom is the only place they can ever get "good training." They've been blinded by past successes to the point that they can't see the value in anything new. To these folks, we wish them only the best. For the rest of us, we're moving on to more effective and efficient methods of learning.

**Beware!** If you do not hold your virtual learners verbally, visually, and kinesthetically accountable, you compromise the quality of the experience and the adoption of new behavior.

**Beware!** If you don't practice, you will most likely fail. Practice, practice, practice! You need to know your content and your technology.

**Beware!** If you do not get your learners' feedback, you will lose valuable information that could be used to improve your virtual classrooms. People like leaving their mark, as long as it is quick and easy to do.

**Beware!** If you plan on going global, you need to dedicate time to this endeavor. It is time-consuming and exhausting. Be prepared to work early in the morning or late at night to accommodate for time-zone differences. You need to also be aware of bizarre infrastructure issues like bandwidth and electricity. But most important, if you don't allow for some degree of local control, you may find that your virtual-classroom content is not effective and won't be adopted.

**Beware!** The biggest cause of failure is a poor launch. You need to be sure you have enough time, energy, and support to propel your virtual-classroom initiative into orbit. Once it's there, you'll still need to spend quality time keeping it there. Otherwise, it will come crashing back to earth in a fiery blaze.

**Beware!** The Learning Explosion is moving faster and faster and shows no signs of slowing. It will never cease to create new learning fragments. If you do not embrace the fact that there is this new mind-set, you will not be prepared for the changes that are constantly occurring.

Remember, you shouldn't be frightened by new ideas. You should be more frightened by old ones.

# The
# Authors
## and The
# Learning
## Explosion

### From Treion

Let me start by sharing one very important—and relevant—demographic about myself. I was born, raised, and schooled in South Africa in the '70s and '80s. This is significant to note because the digital revolution didn't make it to the African continent until the late '80s, early '90s, which may explain why I didn't even get to turn on a computer for the first time until 1995. I was in my first quarter of college when I received an assignment to write a paper...on a computer. I still remember very clearly going to my English 101 teacher and asking if I could submit a handwritten paper instead. After listening to my very well-presented argument, he thought for a second and said no.

I nervously made my way over to the computer lab, where I actually sat at my computer for an hour before I had enough courage to ask the computer lab technician how to turn it on. With a little assistance from him, I not only learned how to turn it on, but also how to find the word processor. Then I looked down at the "QWERTY" keyboard—my new pen—and realized I was in real trouble. At that very moment, I had one of the biggest choices of my entire life to make: adapt or die. I was already far from home, surrounded by loud but nice people with great accents, and faced with so many new and wonderful options. Did I really have to learn how to use a computer?

I chose to adapt. But it took me a long time. That night it took me about 4 hours to write just one page. The next day it took me about 3½ hours to write the second page. Slowly but surely I not only became comfortable with the computer, but proficient with it. I do suffer from one major side effect that came from my late adoption though—I have never learned how to type properly. Instead of elegantly caressing the keys like most people, I end up stabbing at the keys with only a few fingers. Unorthodox? Yes. But despite this obvious disability, I am able to type quite quickly. It's not pretty though. In fact, most people who see me type have to leave the room because it distresses them so much.

The interesting part of this story is that it occurred just 15 years ago. Now I spend most of my days working and writing on a computer.

Being a late adopter only applies to the computer. Since then, I was one of the first PalmPilot users. I am one of those "crazies" who stood in line for an iPhone. I have written much of this book on the iPad. I am an active Facebook and Yammer user, blogger, and tweeter. My daily routine includes receiving and reading industry news via email, blogs, websites, and mobile phone applications. Even though it has only been 15 years since I started this evolutionary journey, I feel like I am keeping up with the pack.

Today I hold a master's degree in instructional design from Utah State University and am FranklinCovey's Chief eLearning Architect, responsible for developing all online-learning initiatives.

I've lived in Utah for the past 15 years, where I spend most of my "offline" time with my talented wife and five amazing children.

## From Matt

 It was 1981; I was in the sixth grade and growing up in the western United States. I was one of only three students from my school selected to learn how to use a personal computer. We had only one. It looked like a large beige typewriter wired to a television set. It sat in the back of the classroom and we all looked at it with curiosity and suspicion. It was an Atari 800 and had 64K of RAM. It was considered a powerhouse by personal-computer standards at the time. But what I didn't know then is that the concept of this one device would change the world forever.

By the time I was 13 years old, my parents bought me something nobody else in the neighborhood had—my very own computer. Friends and neighbors came over to see this novelty. By this time, I was a skilled programmer and had learned how to create games, simple applications, and calculators that enabled me to complete my math homework. It was the forefront of the PC Revolution and I was riding the wave that was getting larger and faster. One day I vividly remember my best friend, who owned an Apple IIe, telling me that some day we would have a gigabyte of memory in our computers. At the time, I couldn't even fathom that concept—yet just last week I purchased a portable external hard drive with an unbelievable terabyte of memory. I'm sure in three years, my *phone* will have a terabyte in it.

Since the sixth grade, I have owned more computers and computer devices than I can remember. I have evolved from saving my work on a cassette tape to floppy discs to hard drives to cloud computing—where this book is being written and saved. In the early 1980s, I would use my 300-baud modem to connect to Bulletin Board Systems (BBS)—the precursor to the Internet—where I would read information shared by other BBS users. It was a simple place to learn about new computer gadgets and programming techniques. It was the beginning of my Learning Explosion.

I now have multiple learning devices at home, and I'm connected through most of the relevant social-networking tools available today. I can't wait to learn what evolutionary path learning is going to take next.

Today I hold an M.B.A. from the University of Utah and spend my days as FranklinCovey's Global Director of Online Learning. This leaves my nights and weekends open for my wife and four children.

# Learning Fragments
## (Notes)

1. Wikipedia.com.

2. ITU World Telecommunication/ICT Indicators Database, "The World in 2010: ICT Facts and Figures." Retrieved with permission from www.itu.int/ITU-D/ict/statistics.

3. JiWire Mobile Audience Insights Report, Q3 2010. Retrieved with permission from http://www.jiwire.com/insights.

4. U.S. Department of Education, Office of Planning, Evaluation, and Policy Development, "Evaluation of Evidence-Based Practices in Online Learning: A Meta-Analysis and Review of Online Learning Studies," Washington, D.C., 2010. Retrieved with permission from www.ed.gov/rschstat/eval/tech/evidence-based-practices/finalreport.pdf.

5. The Corporate Learning Factbook® 2010: "Statistics, Benchmarks and Analysis of the U.S. Corporate Training Market," Bersin & Associates/Karen O'Leonard, January 2010. Available to research members at www.bersin.com/library or for purchase at www.bersin.com/factbook.

6. Pewresearch.org.

7. Astd.org/content/publications.

8. Elearningguild.com.

9. Sloanconsortium.org.

10. broadband.gov.

11. Usdla.org.

12. Data.worldbank.org.

13. Tripit.com.

14. Urbanspoon.com.

15. Teresa Caffe. Go to their website at terramomo.com and read the ratings on urbanspoon.com.

16. Foursquare.com.

17. Genieo.com.

18. Feedly.com.

19. Flipboard. iPad app that allows you to receive RSS feeds and news from several sources, as well as from Twitter and Facebook.

20. Dictionary.com.

21. Curtis Morley's Blog. Read more at www.curtismorley.com.

22. M-W.com. (Merriam-Webster).

23. AcademicEarth.org.

24. Raytheon Features Article. Retrieved with permission from www.raytheon.com/newsroom/feature/rps10_vct.

25. ASTD Learning Circuits, E-Learning Glossary. Get industry definitions from the American Society for Training and Development's glossary. www.astd.org/LC/glossary.

26. LinkedIn.com. Join the Instructional Design & E-Learning Professionals' Group.

27. The eLearning Guild. Go to www.elearningguild.com to become a member, access research, and speak to community members.

28. BlogRank (part of Invesp). BlogRank indexes and collects data for about 20,000 blogs, using over 20+ different factors, including RSS membership, incoming links, Compete Alexa and Technorati ranking, and social sites' popularity. For a list of the top elearning blogs, go to www.invesp.com/blog-rank/elearning.

29. The Corporate Learning Factbook® 2010: "Statistics, Benchmarks and Analysis of the U.S. Corporate Training Market," Bersin & Associates/Karen O'Leonard, January 2010. Available to research members at www.bersin.com/library or for purchase at www.bersin.com/factbook.

30. Smartbrief.com.

31. LinkedIn.com. Join the eLearning Guild Group.

32. Howstuffworks.com.

33. YouTube.com.

34. Indeed.com.

35. CareerBuilder.com.

36. Monster.com.

37. Dictionary.com.

38. EncycloMedia.com.

39. Awesomestories.com.

40. Visionjar.com.

41. Commoncraft.com.

42. Elearninginteractions.com.

43. Vuvox.com.

44. Dipity.com.

45. *Outliers: The Story of Success*. Malcolm Gladwell. Published by Little, Brown and Company, a division of Hachette Book Groups, Inc., 2008.

46. *Talent Is Overrated: What Really Separates World-Class Performers From Everybody Else*. Geoffrey Colvin. Published by the Penguin Group, 2008.

47. Adobe Resource Center. www.adobe.com/resources/acrobatconnect/.

48. WebEx MyResources. http://support.webex.com/support.

49. GoToTraining.com.

50. Citrix Knowledge Center. http://support.citrix.com/.

51. Microsoft LiveMeeting Resource Center. http://office.microsoft.com/en-us/live-meeting/.

52. "20 Things I Learned." www.20thingsilearned.com/#/home.

53. Khan Academy. www.khanacademy.org.

54. Foursquare.com.

55. Gowalla.com.

56. SurveyMonkey.com.

57. Zoomerang.com.

58. Fred Reichheld, *The Ultimate Question*. Harvard Business School Publishing, 2006, Boston.

59. Google Public Data. www.google.com/publicdata/home. Google Public Data gets its information from The World Bank. The primary World Bank collection of development indicators, compiled from officially-recognized international sources. It presents the most current and accurate global development data available, and includes national, regional, and global estimates. Lean more at http://data.worldbank.org/.

60. Speedtest.net.

61. Skype.com.

62. *Crossing the Chasm: Marketing and Selling High-Tech Products to Mainstream Customers*. Geoffrey A. Moore. HarperBusiness, 1999, New York.

# Index

# N

# O

# P

## Acknowledgements

Thanks to all our friends and FranklinCovey family members for bringing this book to fruition. We thank Sean Covey, Shawn Moon, Scott Miller, Boyd Craig, Adam Merrill, Curtis Morley, Sam Bracken, Annie Oswald, Breck England, Jerri Lynn Whatley, Ruth Barker, Leigh Stevens, Catherine Nelson, Terry Lyon, Pam Parkin, Laura Johnson, and Michael Bettin.

Sincere appreciation goes to our core Online Learning team who provided the inspiration and talent for the book: Courtney Mattson, Dave Green, Brad Augustin, and Julie Bednar.

Without the artistic genius from our Creative Services team, this book never would have gone to press. Thank you Jody Karr, Cassidy Back, Sara Thomas, James Boley, RJ Venkatapathy, Michael Elwell, and Riley Onyon (the talented illustrator in the book).

Kudos go to our technical team: Greg Romero, Tyler Staten, Adam Mills, Chris Okelberry, Doug Carter, Blaine Carter, Parker Spendlove, Jon Pham, and our many other technical partners and vendors.

Thanks to Reid Later for his editing help, and Deb Lund for marketing and public-relations assistance.

Special thanks to our families for putting up with us as we wrote this book: Laura, Will, Emma, Josh, and Caroline (the Murdochs); and Soni, Chloe, Layla, Ruby, Gemma, and TJ (the Mullers).

## About FranklinCovey

FranklinCovey (NYSE: FC) is the global consulting and training leader in the areas of strategy execution, customer loyalty, leadership, and individual effectiveness. Clients include 90 percent of the Fortune 100, more than 75 percent of the Fortune 500, and thousands of small and mid-size businesses, as well as numerous government entities and educational institutions. FranklinCovey has 46 direct and licensee offices providing professional services in 147 countries.

FranklinCovey offers training in the following areas:

- Leadership Development
- The 7 Habits®
- Time Management
- Customer Loyalty
- Strategy Consulting
- Communication
- Project Management
- Diversity
- Sales Performance

For more information, go to www.franklincovey.com/tc.

## About FranklinCovey Services

### On-Site Consulting, Training, and Keynotes

Based all over the world, our consultants represent diverse, global industry experience and tailor their delivery to your precise needs—whether consulting, training, or customized keynotes. Our consultants deliver results at any level, from the C-suite to a team or department.

### Client-Facilitator Certification

For organizations seeking cost-effective ways to implement solutions involving large populations of managers and frontline workers, FranklinCovey certifies on-site client facilitators to teach our material and adapt it to your organization's needs. We have certified more than 25,000 client facilitators worldwide.

### Open-Enrollment Public Programs

For organizations needing professional development for a dispersed workforce or education for individuals, FranklinCovey offers nearly 1,200 open-enrollment programs to the public in 120 metropolitan areas throughout the United States. Similar programs are offered throughout the world by our regional and local offices.

### Custom Solutions

When clients have a unique learning or delivery need, FranklinCovey can customize its solutions. We can provide:

- Tailored FranklinCovey training programs.
- Customized planners and binders.
- Specific tools, guides, and other implementation aids.
- Simulations, games, case studies, and other unique learning approaches.

### Content Licensing

For organizations that desire to implement solutions, by division or companywide, in a cost-effective way, FranklinCovey will license your organization to use our content or intellectual property in whatever way you see fit. This provides you with ultimate flexibility and scalability.

## FranklinCovey Online Learning

FranklinCovey's Online Learning practice provides a library of products and consulting services to help you reach more people with effective and high-quality training.

LiveClicks webinar workshops put the high-quality instruction of FranklinCovey in-person training into convenient online workshops. LiveClicks webinar workshops are led by our certified instructors, or yours, and are presented live online in two-hour modules. Engaging and interactive, LiveClicks webinar workshops offer compelling content and award-winning videos. Learn more at: **www.franklincovey.com/liveclicks.**

Help teams take action for increased performance with FranklinCovey InSights. InSights are short, Web-based, video-rich learning modules based on core competencies, delivered in the course of regularly held meetings by your own managers or leaders. Each InSights module starts with an engaging video, followed by powerful discussion questions. Our online forum and goal-tracking tool further help teams learn and develop. Learn more at: **www.franklincovey.com/insights.**

Develop effective employees and build cohesive teams, no matter what the person's role, with *The 7 Habits of Highly Effective People—Interactive Edition.* Based on the best-selling business book and our world-class effectiveness workshops, *The 7 Habits Interactive Edition* is a three-hour, self-paced online experience, with an optional one-day live session available for a blended-learning experience. Learn more at: **www.franklincovey.com/the7habitsinteractive.**

For more information, contact a FranklinCovey Online Learning Specialist at: 1-888-576-1776.

# The Learning Explosion Resource Sites

| Resource | Description |
|---|---|
| Twitter.com | Twitter can be an effective learning tool. We use it as a means of discovering and sharing learning fragments. twitter.com/learningexplosn |
| Twitter Hashtag | Whenever you discover a new learning fragment, just add #LFRAG to your tweet. This way #LFRAG becomes an online location for sharing learning fragments with each other. Even if you are not an active tweeter, you can still go to twitter.com and search #LFRAG to view what others are discovering. |
| Blog | Read our blog posts as we look at the future of learning, interesting trends, and relevant learning news. thelearningexplosion.com |
| Book Website | Access some of the Learning Explosion Action Plans, plus you can see our rolling Twitter feed at franklincovey.com/thelearningexplosion. |
| Facebook | If Facebook is your social-media preference, then like "The Learning Explosion" and follow us there. |
| LinkedIn | To engage Matt and Treion in conversation, please connect with us on LinkedIn.com. linkedin.com/in/mattmurdoch linkedin.com/in/treionmuller |